Silke Wustmann | Christian Setzepfandt

Frankfurter ArchitekTour

Die 100 wichtigsten Gebäude der Mainmetropole aus allen Epochen und sechs thematische Stadtrundgänge

B VERLAG

Bildnachweis:

Frankfurter Spielbetrieb:
Gebäude 03, 22, 29, 39, 40, 55, 67, 72, 73, 76, 83, 91, Tour 4, Tour 5, Tour 6

B3 Verlag: Gebäude 07, 23, 33, 37, 52, 59, 60, 90, Tour 2, Tour 3, Tour 6

HistoCom GmbH: Gebäude 48

Dietmar Strauß: Gebäude 86:

Der komplette Bildnachweis ist unter www.bedrei.de/frankfurter-architektour einsehbar.

Impressum

Silke Wustmann; Christian Setzepfandt: Frankfurter ArchitekTour
Die 100 wichtigsten Gebäude der Mainmetropole aus allen Epochen und sieben thematische Stadtrundgänge.

Gebäude 1–54 und Touren 1, 2, 4, 5: Silke Wustmann
Gebäude 55–100 und Touren 3, 6: Christian Setzepfandt

Weitere Titel des B3 Verlages unter www.bedrei.de

Gestaltung, Satz und Umschlag: vierzwei, Frankfurt am Main
Umschlagmotiv: iStockphoto, unten B3 Verlag, Frankfurt am Main
Übersetzung: Darlene Waldschmidt-Sematat, Frankfurt am Main
Printed in Germany

ISBN 978-3-938783-14-6

GEBÄUDE

TOUREN

Translation:

Adresse	– **Adress**	**Architekt**	– **Architect**
Erbauung	– **Edification**	**Rekonstruktion**	– **Reconstruction**
Stadtteil	– **District**	**Umbau**	– **Conversion**
Wiederaufbau	– **Rebuilding**		

Liebe Leserinnen und Leser,

das Stadtbild von Frankfurt am Main wird heute fast ausschließlich mit den Bürotürmen der Skyline in Verbindung gebracht. Sicherlich sind die Hochhäuser zu einem Markenzeichen der Stadt geworden, aber sie sind nur ein Aspekt ihrer vielseitigen Architektur, für die die immense Zerstörung im Zweiten Weltkrieg eine entscheidende Zäsur darstellt.

Dieses Buch möchte Ihnen die „100 wichtigsten Gebäude aus allen Epochen" vorstellen – ein großer Anspruch, das ist uns bewusst. Die Auswahl ist uns entsprechend schwergefallen. Wir haben lange und heiß diskutiert, bevor wir uns endgültig ent-schieden haben, welche Bauwerke aufgenommen werden sollten. Ein gewisses Maß an Subjektivität sei uns dabei zugestanden. Vielleicht werden Sie bei der Durchsicht der Einzeldarstellungen das eine oder andere Gebäude vermissen, das wir Ihrer Ansicht nach unbedingt hätten aufnehmen müssen. Sollte dies der Fall sein, schauen Sie bitte einmal in unseren thematisch gegliederten „ArchitekTouren" im zweiten Teil des Buches nach. Dort finden zahlreiche weitere Bauten Erwähnung, sodass letztlich doch eine gewisse Vollständigkeit erreicht werden konnte.

Vorwort

Die „Frankfurter ArchitekTour" richtet sich nicht an ausgewiesene Kenner der Materie, sondern möchte Einheimische und Besucher, Laien mit und ohne Vorkenntnisse in knapper und allgemein verständlicher Form über die baulichen Besonderheiten Frankfurts informieren.
Durch die Anordnung der Gebäude im Buch nach Ihrer Entstehungszeit, ergibt sich auch ein visueller Eindruck der Stadtentwicklung.

Entdecken Sie mit diesem Buch die architektonische Vielseitigkeit der Mainmetropole!

Viel Spaß dabei wünschen

Silke Wustmann & Christian Setzepfandt

01 | Justinuskirche

Die im Kern karolingische Basilika ist das älteste erhaltene Gebäude Frankfurts und eine der ältesten Kirchen Deutschlands überhaupt. In der Frühromanik wurde sie erhöht, ab 1441 erhielt sie im Auftrag des Antoniterordens ein zusätzliches Nordschiff mit figürlichem Portal und den spätgotischen Hochchor. Im Inneren sind unter anderem die originalen korinthischen Säulen des 9. Jhs. mit ihren reichen Kapitellen und die prachtvolle Barockorgel sehenswert.

St. Justinus' Church *The core of the basilica is Carolingian; it is the oldest surviving building in Frankfurt and one of the oldest churches in Germany as a whole. The height of the church was increased in the early Romanesque period. As of 1441 an additional nave with a figured portal was built on the northern side and the late Gothic elevated choir was added at the request of the Hospital Brothers of St. Anthony. The interior is well worth a visit, among other things because of the original 9th century Corinthian columns with their richly decorated capitals and the splendid baroque organ.*

Adresse: Justinusplatz 3 | **Stadtteil:** Höchst
Erbauung: um 850 geweiht; Umbauten: um 1090; ab 1441

Saalhof | 02

Der romanische Saalhof wurde als Ersatz für die karolingische Königspfalz vor dem Dom in der Stauferzeit (spätestens unter Friedrich I. Barbarossa) in schlichten Formen errichtet. Teile des Wohntraktes mit rekonstruierten Biforienfenstern auf beiden Seiten des Festraums – „des Reiches Saal", daher der Name des Gebäudes – sind erhalten, ebenso ein Turm und die Palastkapelle mit Apsiserker. Der Saalhof wird heute vom Historischen Museum Frankfurt genutzt.

SAALHOF *The Romanesque Saalhof was constructed as a simple complex to replace the Carolingian „Königspfalz" (royal palace) in front of the Cathedral during the Staufer dynasty (at the latest under Frederick I Barbarossa). Parts of the residential section with reconstructed biforium windows on both sides of the feasting hall – "des Reiches Saal" (Hall of the Kingdom), which gave rise to the name of the building – have survived, as have one tower and the palace chapel with an apse alcove. Today the "Saalhof" is used by the Historical Museum of Frankfurt.*

Adresse: Saalgasse 19 | **Stadtteil:** Altstadt | **Erbauung:** um 1140–1160

Die kleine königliche Hofkapelle, im 13. Jh. zur zweischiffigen Halle ausgebaut, erhielt ihre heutige Gestalt im 15. Jh., als sie in städtischen Besitz kam und zur Ratskirche umgewandelt wurde. Friedberger verlängerte den bereits achteckig angelegten Turm, Schopfheim erhöhte das Langhaus mit dem charakteristischen Walmdach und Lich schuf die signifikante spätgotische Dachgalerie mit der Maßwerkbrüstung und den oktogonalen Ecktürmchen.

OLD CHURCH OF ST. NICHOLAS

The small chapel of the royal court, which was enlarged into a two-nave hall in the 13th century, was given its present appearance in the 15th century, when it

03 | Alte Nikolaikirche

became the property of the city and was transformed into the "Ratskirche" (the town councillors' church). Friedberger made the tower, which was already octagonal, higher. Schopfheim raised the height of the nave with the characteristic hipped roof and Lich created the significant late Gothic roof gallery with the tracery balustrade and the octagonal corner towers.

Adresse: Römerberg
Stadtteil: Altstadt
Erbauung: um 1150; Umbauten: 1270 bis 1290; um 1440–1467
Architekten: Eberhard Friedberger, Bartholomäus von Schopfheim, Hans von Lich (Umbau)

Staufenmauer | 04

Die aus Bruchsteinen bestehende romanische Stadtmauer ist 75 Meter lang und zwischen sechs und acht Metern hoch. Die Innenseite wurde durch unregelmäßige Blendbögen verstärkt, die ebenso wie die Auflagen des ehemaligen Wehrgangs noch erkennbar sind. Nach der Stadterweiterung ab 1333 wies man den Frankfurter Juden das jenseitige Areal zur Besiedelung zu (ab 1462 als Ghetto). Nach dem sogenannten Großen Judenbrand von 1711 musste die Mauer teilweise ersetzt werden.

STAUFER WALL *The Romanesque city wall built of quarry stone is 75 metres long and between six and eight metres high. The inside was reinforced with irregular blind arches, which are still visible as are the supports of the former parapet walk. After the city was enlarged as of 1333, the area beyond the wall was designated for settlement by Frankfurt's Jews (since 1462 as a ghetto). After the so-called "Großer Judenbrand" (Great Jewish Fire) in 1711, parts of the wall had to be replaced.*

Adresse: Fahrgasse / Töngesgasse | **Stadtteil:** Altstadt
Erbauung: um 1180; Erneuerung: 1711

Die dreischiffige spätromanische Basilika mit ihren Zwillingstürmen wurde, wohl nach einem Entwurf von Gerthener, ab ca. 1425 von einer spätgotischen Hallenkirche mit polygonalem Hochchor überfangen. Bingen und sein Nachfolger Baltz fügten im 16. Jh. die beiden neuen Außenschiffe an. Die ehemaligen Nordportale des 13. Jhs. von Engelbertus und das sogenannte Salvatorchörlein von Baltz um 1515 sind Meisterwerke der Bildhauerkunst.

St. Leonhard

The three-nave basilica with its twin towers, which was probably designed by Gerthener, was overlaid with a late Gothic hall church including a polygonal

05 | St. Leonhard

elevated choir as of approx. 1425. In the 16th century, Bingen and his successor Baltz added the two new exterior naves. The former northern portals from the 13th century by Engelbertus and the so-called "Salvatorchörlein" (Little Chapel of the Saviour) by Baltz dating to around 1515 are masterpieces of the art of sculpture.

Adresse: Am Leonhardstor / Alte Mainzer Gasse
Stadtteil: Altstadt
Erbauung: ab 1219; Umbauten: um 1425; 1505–1523
Architekten: vermutlich Madern Gerthener (Umbau); Hans von Bingen, Hans Baltz (Umbau)

Der Dominikanerorden ließ sich 1233 am östlichen Stadtrand nieder und errichtete eine gotische Klosteranlage mit dreischiffiger Hallenkirche. Sie erhielt im 15. Jh. nach dem Entwurf Östreichers einen rippengewölbten Polygonalchor, der heute noch erhalten ist. Die barockisierten Konventsgebäude wurden im Zweiten Weltkrieg zerstört und auf ihren mittelalterlichen Fundamenten von Scheinpflug modern ersetzt. Heute ist hier der Evangelische Regionalverband untergebracht.

Dominican Monastery and Church of the Holy Spirit

The Dominican Order settled on the eastern edge of the city in 1233 and

Dominikanerkloster und Heilig-Geist-Kirche | 06

constructed a Gothic monastery complex with a three-nave hall church. In the 15th century, a polygonal choir with a ribbed vault designed by Östreicher was added and it has survived to this day. The convent building decorated in the baroque style was destroyed during World War II and Scheinpflug replaced it with a modern structure that was erected on the medieval foundations. Today it houses the Protestant Regional Association.

Adresse: Kurt-Schumacher-Straße 23
Stadtteil: Altstadt
Erbauung: ab 1233; Umbauten: 1470–1472; nach 1679; Wiederaufbau: 1955–1960
Architekten: Jörg Östreicher (Umbau); Gustav Scheinpflug (Wiederaufbau)

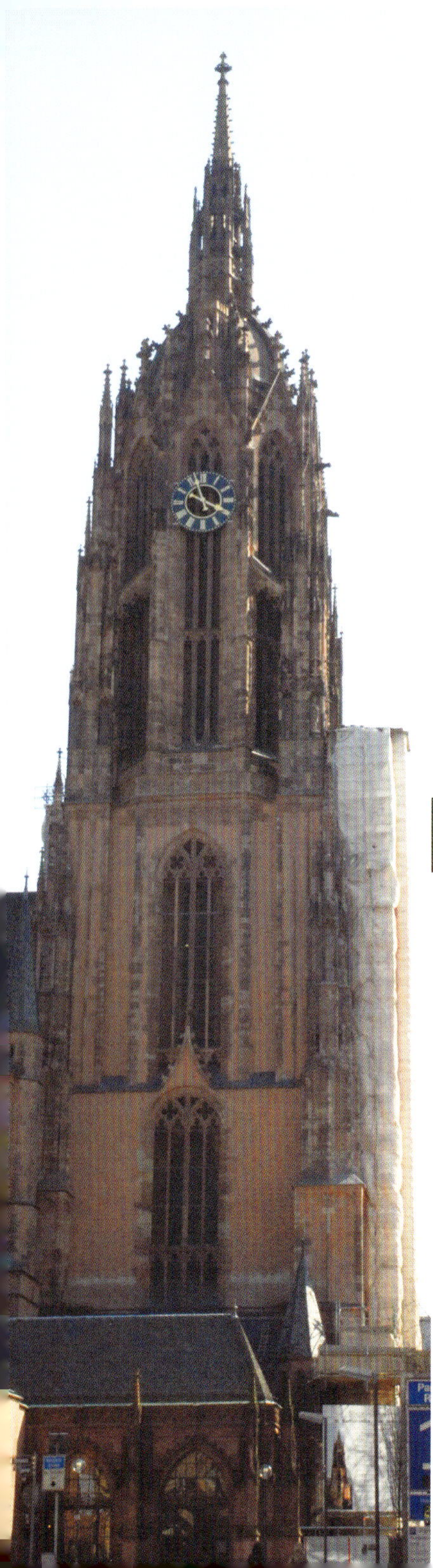

Über Vorgängerbauten aus merowingischer und karolingischer Zeit entwickelte sich seit dem 13. Jh. die städtische Kirche St. Bartholomäus. Der bis heute vorherrschende spätgotische Eindruck liegt an den im 15. Jh. vorgenommenen Ausbauten. Der damals begonnene Westturm von Gerthener blieb unvollendet und wurde erst nach dem Dombrand von 1867 durch Denzinger fertiggestellt.
Der Dom war seit 1356 Wahlstätte und seit 1562 Krönungsort der deutschen Könige und Kaiser.

CATHEDRAL OF ST. BARTHOLOMEUS

The city Church of St. Bartholomeus has developed since the 13th century on the site of previous structures dating back

07 | Dom St. Bartholomäus

to the Merovingian and Carolingian periods. The late Gothic appearance that predominates today is the result of the additions that were executed in the 15th century. The west tower by Gerthener, which was comenced at that time, remained unfinished and it was not until after the Cathedral fire that it was completed by Denzinger in 1867. As of 1356 the Cathedral was the venue of the elections and as of 1562 it was the place where the coronations of the German kings and emperors were held.

Adresse: Domplatz | **Stadtteil:** Altstadt
Erbauung: 1239 geweiht;
Umbauten: 1415–1514; 1869–1880
Architekten: Madern Gerthener (Umbau);
Franz Josef von Denzinger (Umbau)

Erst nach über zwei Jahrhunderten Wildwuchs wurde in der Spätgotik ein einheitlicher Klosterkomplex geschaffen. Am Umbau der bisherigen Saalkirche war damals höchstwahrscheinlich auch Gerthener beteiligt. Die Anlage wurde nach der Kriegszerstörung vereinfacht wieder aufgebaut und später um einen Museumsneubau für das Archäologische Museum ergänzt. Im Kreuzgang befindet sich das (leider beschädigte) größte Wandgemälde nördlich der Alpen, von Jörg Ratgeb (1514–1518).

CARMELITE MONASTERY AND CARMELITE CHURCH ST. MARIA

It was only after over two centuries of uncontrolled growth that a unified monastery

Karmeliterkloster und Karmeliterkirche St. Maria | 08

complex was created in the late Gothic period. It is highly probable that at that time Gerthener was also involved in the remodelling work on the church, which had been a single-nave hall church until then. After the destruction during the War, the complex was rebuilt in simpler form and was later supplemented by a new museum building for the Archaeological Museum. The largest mural painting north of the Alps - by Jörg Ratgeb (1514-1518) - can be found in the cloisters, unfortunately it is damaged.

Adresse: Karmelitergasse 1–5
Stadtteil: Altstadt | **Erbauung:** ab 1246; Umbau: um 1460–1520; Wiederaufbau: 1955–1957; Museumsneubau: 1987–1989
Architekten: Madern Gerthener (Umbau); Josef Paul Kleihues (Museumsneubau)

09 | Haus Schellgasse

Durch den dendrochronologischen Befund eines darin verwendeten Eichenholzbalkens kann das im heutigen Stadtbild leicht zu übersehende Häuschen zweifelsfrei auf das Jahr 1291 datiert werden. Damit ist es der älteste Fachwerkbau Frankfurts und gehört sogar zu den ältesten in Deutschland. An ihm lässt sich die Wohnsituation der einfachen Bevölkerung im Mittelalter ablesen. Nach seiner Renovierung dient es nun dem Verein „Freunde Frankfurts" als Versammlungsort.

SCHELLGASSE HOUSE *According to the results of the dendrochronological examination of an oak beam that was used in it, the year of construction of the small building, which is easy to overlook in today's urban landscape, is incontrovertibly 1291. That makes it the oldest half-timbered structure in Frankfurt and even one of the oldest in all of Germany. It illustrates the living situation of the simple folk in the Middle Ages. Since its renovation "Freunde Frankfurts", an association dedicated to preserving Frankfurt's heritage, has been using it as a meeting place.*

Adresse: Schellgasse 8 (Walter-Kolb-Straße) | **Stadtteil:** Sachsenhausen
Erbauung: 1291; Erneuerung: 1986–1988

Deutschordenshaus und Deutschordenskirche St. Maria | 10

Der seit dem 13. Jh. in Sachsenhausen ansässige Deutsche Orden ließ im 18. Jh. seine alten Gebäude durch eine eindrucksvolle barocke Dreiflügelanlage ersetzen, deren Fassade durch das rittergeschmückte Hauptportal akzentuiert wird. Der kleinen gotischen Saalkirche wurde eine barocke Front vorgeblendet, um einen harmonischen Gesamteindruck zu erhalten. Im Deutschordenshaus ist inzwischen das Ikonen-Museum der Stadt Frankfurt – Stiftung Dr. Schmidt-Voigt untergebracht.

St. Mary's Church of the Teutonic Order and Preceptory of the Teutonic Order

In the 18th century the Teutonic Order of Knights - which had maintained a presence in Sachsenhausen as of the 13th century - had its old buildings replaced by a baroque triple-wing complex with a façade that is accentuated by the main portal decorated with figures of knights. A baroque front was added to the small Gothic single-nave hall church in order to achieve a harmonious overall impression. In the meantime, the Preceptory of the Teutonic Order is the Icon Museum of the City of Frankfurt Stadt Frankfurt, Stiftung Dr. Schmidt-Voigt.

Adresse: Brückenstraße 3–5 | **Stadtteil:** Sachsenhausen | **Erbauung:** 1309 geweiht (Kirche); Umbauten: 1709–1715 (Ordenshaus); 1747–1751 (Kirche)
Architekten: Daniel Kayser (Umbau Ordenshaus); Ferdinand Kirchmeyer (Umbau Kirche)

11 | Liebfrauenkirche

Die auf eine patrizische Stiftung Anfang des 14. Jhs. zurückgehende gotische Hallenkirche erhielt im 15. Jh. die südliche Schaufassade mit dem wahrscheinlich von Gerthener stammenden sehenswerten Dreikönigsportal, das wegen des klassizistischen Vorbaus durch Rumpf heute im Inneren des Gebäudes liegt. Der Chor wurde Anfang des 16. Jhs. nach dem Plan Östreichers zu einem steileren Polygon umgebaut. Liebfrauen ist seit 1917 Klosterkirche des angegliederten Kapuzinerordens.

CHURCH OF OUR LADY *The Gothic Hall church was built by a patrician foundation at the beginning of the 14th century. In the 15th century, the southern "window-dressing" façade was added including the impressive "Dreikönigsportal" (Three Kings Portal), which was probably designed by Gerthener. Today it is located within the building because of the classicistic porch addition by Rumpf. At the beginning of the 16th century, the choir was altered to form a steeper polygon. Since 1917 "Liebfrauenkirche" has been a monastery church of the associated Capuchin Order.*

Adresse: Liebfrauenstraße 2–4 | **Stadtteil:** Altstadt
Erbauung: 1344 geweiht; Umbauten: um 1425; 1506–1509; 1824
Architekten: Madern Gerthener (Umbau); Jörg Östreicher (Umbau); Friedrich Rumpf (Umbau)

Die bereits Ende des 14. Jhs. gestiftete Peterskapelle wurde 1452 zur Pfarrkirche der Neustadt erhoben. Sie galt als Grablege der Patrizier, während die restliche Bevölkerung auf dem ringsum entstandenen Kirchhof bestattet wurde. Er war seit der Reformation bis zu seiner Schließung 1828 zentraler Begräbnisort der Protestanten, z.B. von Goethes Eltern (Grabmäler noch vorhanden). Die mittelalterliche Kirche wurde im 19. Jh. durch eine neugotische ersetzt. St. Peter ist heute Jugendkulturkirche.

CHURCH OF ST. PETER AND ST. PETER'S CHURCHYARD

The "Peterskapelle" (Chapel of St. Peter), which was already founded at the end of

Peterskirche und Peterskirchhof | 12

the 14th century, was made the parish church of the "Neustadt" (new town) district in 1452. It was the burial place of the patricians, while the rest of the populace were buried in the surrounding churchyard that grew up around it. Since the reformation until it was closed in 1828, it was the central burial site for Protestants, for example the parents of Goethe (their tombs are still there). The medieval church was replaced by a neo-Gothic one in the 19th century. Today St. Peter is a church with a youth culture focus.

Adresse: Bleichstr. 33 | **Stadtteil:** Innenstadt
Erbauung: 1393 gestiftet (Kirche); ab 1452 (Friedhof); Neubau: 1892–1895 (Kirche)
Architekten: August Georg Dinklage, Hans Grisebach (Neubau Kirche)

13 | Leinwandhaus

Wahrscheinlich entwarf Gerthener Ende des 14. Jhs. das öffentliche Gebäude der Spätgotik mit Ladenarkaden im Erdgeschoss, Kreuzstockfenstern und Figurenkonsolen im Obergeschoss, dekorativem Wehrumgang und steilem Walmdach. Gedacht als Lager- und Verkaufsstätte für Stoffe, diente es in den folgenden Jahrhunderten ganz unterschiedlichen Zwecken und beherbergt nun das caricatura museum frankfurt – Museum für Komische Kunst.

HOUSE OF LINEN *It is likely that Gerthener designed the late Gothic public building at the end of the 14th century: it has shop arcades on the ground floor, crossbar windows and figured corbels on the upper level, a decorative battlement parapet and a steep hipped roof. It was planned as a place for storing and selling fabrics. In subsequent centuries it has been used for widely differing purposes. At present it houses the "caricatura museum Frankfurt" – the Museum for Comic Art.*

Adresse: Weckmarkt 17 | **Stadtteil:** Altstadt | **Erbauung:** 1399 vollendet
Architekt: vermutlich Madern Gerthener

Von den über 50 Wehrtürmen, die im Zusammenhang mit der spätgotischen Stadtbefestigung entstanden, war er der aufwendigste und blieb daher als einziger vom Abriss verschont. 1400 von Mengoz begonnen, wurde er von Gerthener fertiggestellt. Der zylindrische Schaft sitzt auf einem kubischen Sockel und endet in einem spitzen Kegel, der von einem Zinnenkranz mit vier Erkertürmchen eingefasst wird. Der Verlauf des alten Wehrgangs ist auf der Stadtseite heute noch sichtbar.

ESCHENHEIMER TOWER

Of the 60 defence towers that were built as part of the late Gothic city fortifications, this was the most lavish. That is why it is

Eschenheimer Turm | 14

the only one that has escaped being torn down. Mengoz commenced the work in 1400, and it was completed by Gerthener. The cylindrical shaft rests on a cubical plinth and ends in a pointed cone, which is framed by crenellation including four turrets. On the side facing the city the location of the old battlement parapet is still visible.

Adresse: Eschenheimer Tor
Stadtteil: Innenstadt
Erbauung: 1400–1428
Architekten: Klaus Mengoz, Madern Gerthener

15 | Rathaus Römer

Das 1322 erstmals erwähnte Bürgerhaus „Zum Römer“ und sein Hinterhaus wurden 1405 vom Rat erworben und unter Königshofen und Sparre für kommunale Zwecke umgebaut. Im Lauf der nächsten fünf Jahrhunderte wurden neun Nachbarhäuser hinzugekauft und dem Rathauskomplex einverleibt. Die berühmte Dreigiebelfassade zum Römerberg wurde Ende des 19. Jhs. nach dem Entwurf Meckels im neugotischen Stil dekoriert. Nach dem Zweiten Weltkrieg erfolgte ein zeittypischer Wiederaufbau.

CITY HALL *The first documentation of the public hall called "Zum Römer" was in 1322. The city council purchased the rear building in 1405 and it was converted for use by the city under Königshofen and Sparre. In the course of the subsequent five centuries, nine neighbouring buildings were additionally purchased and incorporated into the city hall complex. The famous triple gable façade of "Zum Römerberg" was decorated in the Neo-Gothic style at the end of the 19th century according to a design by Meckel. After World War II it was reconstructed in a style typical of the period.*

Adresse: Römerberg 19–27 | **Stadtteil:** Altstadt | **Erbauung:** 1405–1408; Umbau: 1896/97; Wiederaufbau: 1950–1955 | **Architekten:** Friedrich von Königshofen, Wigel Sparre; Max Meckel (Umbau); Otto Apel, Rudolf Letocha, William Rohrer und Martin Herdt (Wiederaufbau)

Der Turm wurde zunächst als Sicherung des Fahrtors und der Stadtmauer am Anker- und Stapelplatz der Schiffe errichtet; nachdem 1489 im ersten Stock das Rentenamt eingerichtet wurde, das die Hafen- und Zollgebühren erhob, erhielt er seinen noch heute gebräuchlichen Namen. Der Dachabschluss erinnert stark an den des Eschenheimer Turms. Durch die Aufschüttung des Mainkais im 19. Jh. versank ein Teil des Bauwerks, was seine ehemals schlanken Proportionen stark beeinträchtigt.

RENTENTURM

This tower was originally built to secure the gate called "Fahrtor" and the city wall at the anchorage ground and

Rententurm | 16

stacking ground for ships. Its name, which is still in common use, is derived from the "Rentamt" (fiscal office), the authority that levied the harbour and customs duties which was installed on the second level in 1489.
The roof design is very similar to that of the Eschenheimer Tower. When the embankment of the Main was raised in the 19th century, part of the structure was buried, which had a negative effect on its formerly slender proportions.

Adresse: Mainkai / Fahrtor
Stadtteil: Altstadt
Erbauung: 1456
Architekt: Eberhard Friedberger

Das ehemalige Wohn- und Geschäftshaus der aus Köln eingewanderten Familie Melem und heutiger Sitz des Frankfurter Kunstvereins besteht aus Mainsandstein und Basalttuff. Die Fassade setzt voll auf Repräsentation, besonders der zinnenbewehrte Umgang und die Ecktürme des hohen Walmdaches mit ihrer rein dekorativen Funktion. Das durch den Krieg stark in Mitleidenschaft gezogene Gebäude verfügt noch über das originale spätgotische Netzgewölbe der ehemaligen Einfahrt.

STONE HOUSE

The former residential and commercial building belonging to the Melem family, who had moved there from Cologne,

17 | Steinernes Haus

was built of Main sandstone and basalt tuff. Today it houses the "Frankfurter Kunstverein" (Frankfurt Art Association). The façade is entirely focussed on making a prestigious impression; in particular, the pinnacle bordered parapet and the corner turrets of the high hipped roof are purely decorative. The building was severely damaged during the war, but the original late Gothic reticulated vaulting above the former gateway entrance has survived.

Adresse: Markt 44
Stadtteil: Altstadt
Erbauung: 1464; Wiederaufbau: 1957–1960

An das im 14. und 15. Jh. geschaffene System von Landwehren, die aus Wall und Graben bestanden und durch in Abständen aufgestellte Türme gesichert wurden, erinnert südlich des Mains nur noch diese spätgotische Warte mit Schießscharten in Schlüssellochform und verschiefertem Fachwerkdachgeschoss. Innerhalb des aus gleicher Zeit stammenden Wehrhofs sind Reste eines barocken Forst- und Geleitshauses vorhanden, in dem heute ein Restaurant untergebracht ist.

Sachsenhausen Look-out Tower

In the 14th and 15th centuries a system of defensive dykes consisting of banks and trenches was created and secured

Sachsenhäuser Warte | 18

by towers placed at intervals. The only vestige of that system south of the Main is this late Gothic look-out tower with keyhole-shaped arrow slits and a half-timbered attic sheathed in slate cladding. Today a restaurant is located within the fortified estate that dates back to the same period, in a building that is what remains of a baroque forester's lodge and a road safety escort fee collection point.

Adresse: Darmstädter Landstraße 279
Stadtteil: Sachsenhausen
Erbauung: 1470–1471 (Turm); Erneuerung: 1552 (Turm); 1767 (Forsthaus)
Architekt: Johann Andreas Liebhardt (Forsthaus)

19 | Haus Wertheim

Als einziges von über 1.000 Fachwerkhäusern des Altstadtkerns überstand das Haus Wertheim das Bombardement vom 22. auf den 23. März 1944. Es ist ein repräsentatives Renaissancegebäude ortstypischer Ausprägung. Die über den Erdgeschossarkaden aus Sandstein doppelt auskragenden Obergeschosse bestehen aus einem aufwendigen Holzgefüge mit schön verzierten Eckpfosten. Die großen Gauben des schiefergedeckten Daches gehen allerdings auf das 20. Jh. zurück.

WERTHEIM BUILDING *"Haus Wertheim" is the only one of the over 1,000 half-timbered houses in the old medieval centre that survived the bomb that rained on the city from March 22nd to 23rd, 1944. It is a prestigious Renaissance building in the style that was typical of the city. The two upper levels projecting out in steps above the ground floor arcades made of sandstone consist of a complicated post and beam system with beautifully decorated corner posts. However, the large dormers inserted in the slate roof are only 20th century.*

Adresse: Fahrtor 1 | **Stadtteil:** Altstadt | **Erbauung:** um 1600

Anstelle der mittelalterlichen Doppelkapelle, in der 1522 die erste reformatorische Predigt Frankfurts gehalten wurde, entstand im 17. Jh. auch die erste auf die Bedürfnisse der protestantischen Liturgie zugeschnittene Kirche der Stadt. Architektonisch mischen sich hier gotische und barocke Stilelemente, wie sich beispielsweise an der Turmbekrönung ablesen lässt. Während die Fassade beim Wiederaufbau rekonstruiert wurde, wurde das Innere sehr schlicht ausgestaltet.

CHURCH OF ST. CATHERINE

In the 17th century the first church in the city that was tailored to the requirements of Protestant liturgy was built to replace

Katharinenkirche | 20

the medieval double chapel where the first Protestant sermon was preached in Frankfurt in 1522. The architecture is a mixture of Gothic and baroque stylistic elements, which can be recognised in the design used for the top of the tower, for example. Whereas the façade was restored during reconstruction, the interior has been left very austere.

Adresse: Zeil 131
Stadtteil: Innenstadt
Erbauung: 1678–1681
Architekt: Melchior Heßler

21 | Bernusbau

Direkt neben dem Rententurm und ihn regelrecht umschließend entstand im 18. Jh. anstelle der Flussmauer der barocke Stadtpalast im Auftrag der aus Hanau eingewanderten niederländischen Kaufmannsfamilie Bernus. Jedes Geschoss weist unterschiedliche Fensterdekorationen auf, das Gebäude wird von Dachgauben mit schön ausgestalteten Zwerchhäusern aus Sandstein bekrönt. Heute ist der Bernusbau Bestandteil des Historischen Museums Frankfurt.

BERNUS BUILDING *This baroque city palace was constructed in the 18th century for the Bernus family, Dutch merchants who had moved to Frankfurt from Hanau. It is located directly next to the "Rententurm" and effectively encircles it. Different window decorations have been used for each storey; the building is crowned by roof dormers with beautifully fashioned gable lucarnes made of sandstone. Today the "Bernusbau" is part of the Historical Museum of Frankfurt.*

Adresse: Fahrtor / Mainkai | **Stadtteil:** Altstadt | **Erbauung:** 1715–1717
Architekt: Bernhard Kirn

Petrihaus | 22

Das Fachwerkhaus Johann Petris kam 1819 in den Besitz des Bankiers Georg Brentano, der es nach Anregungen Schinkels zu einem klassizistischen Schweizerhäuschen mit überkragendem Dach, Schnitzgiebel und umlaufendem Balkon umbauen ließ. Das Petrihaus ist als Detail des Brentanoparks zu verstehen, der ehemals fast 14 Hektar umfasste. Das stark verfallene Gebäude wurde liebevoll restauriert, beherbergt heute ein kleines Museum und ist von einem romantischen Garten umgeben.

PETRI HOUSE *The banker Georg Brentano purchased the half-timbered house of Johann Petri in 1819. He had it transformed into a classicistic Swiss chalet according to a design suggested by Schinkel, with a projecting roof, carved gables and a balcony encircling the building. The "Petrihaus" is a decorative element in the Brentanopark, which formerly encompassed almost 14 hectares. The building had deteriorated severely.*
However, it has been lovingly restored. Today it houses a small museum and is surrounded by a romantic garden.

Adresse: Am Rödelheimer Wehr 15 | **Stadtteil:** Rödelheim
Erbauung: um 1720; Umbau: 1820; Sanierung: 1999–2000
Architekten: Karl Friedrich Schinkel (Umbau); Claus Giel (Sanierung)

23 | Holzhausenschlösschen

Auf den Fundamenten der „Holzhausenschen Oede“, die in der Renaissance zum Landhaus ausgebaut worden war, errichtete man dieses bezaubernde Wasserschlösschen, das bis auf den heutigen Tag über eine steinerne Bogenbrücke erreichbar ist. Der schlichte Rechteckbau ist sehr schmal. Sein auffälligstes Merkmal ist das Mansarddach mit dem kleinen Oberlicht, in Frankfurt „Belvederchen“ genannt. Der Zweite Weltkrieg hat die Innenausstattung des Gebäudes zerstört.

LITTLE HOLZHAUSEN CASTLE *This delightful small castle surrounded by a moat was built on the foundations of the "Holzhausensche Oede", which was enlarged into a country house in the Renaissance period. Even today access provided is by way of an arched stone bridge. The unadorned rectangular structure is very narrow. The most conspicuous attribute is the mansard roof surmounted by a small roof light, which is called "Belvederchen" (Little Belvedere) in Frankfurt. The interior fittings of the building were destroyed during Second World War.*

Adresse: Justinianstraße 5 | **Stadtteil:** Nordend | **Erbauung:** 1727–1729
Architekt: Louis Rémy de la Fosse

Hauptwache | 24

Seit 1671 war hier eine Station der Frankfurter Bürgerwehr lokalisiert, die im Barock einen repräsentativen Neubau erhielt. Das niedrige Gebäude beherbergte im Erdgeschoss das Wachlokal, während in den Zimmern des ersten Stocks die vornehmeren und in den Verliesen des Kellers die weniger privilegierten Gefangenen untergebracht waren. Auffällig ist das Giebelrelief mit Stadtwappen und Trophäen (Kopie). Die Hauptwache wurde 1968 für den U-Bahn-Bau um einige Meter versetzt.

MAIN GUARD STATION *As of 1671 Frankfurt's city militia was stationed here. A prestigious new building was erected in the baroque period. The low building housed the guardroom on the ground floor, while the rooms on the first upper level were used to accommodate higher-class prisoners and the less privileged ones were relegated to the dungeons in the cellar. The gable relief with the city's coat of arms and trophies (a copy) is striking. In 1968 the "Hauptwache" was moved over a few metres because of construction of the underground railway.*

Adresse: An der Hauptwache 15 | **Stadtteil:** Innenstadt | **Erbauung:** 1729–1730
Architekt: Johann Jakob Samhaimer

25 | Palais Thurn und Taxis

Fürst Anselm Franz von Thurn und Taxis ließ die wichtigste kaiserliche Poststation im Alten Reich als spätbarocke Dreiflügelanlage errichten. Nach den verheerenden Kriegszerstörungen blieben von dem von 1816 bis 1866 als Sitz des Deutschen Bundestages genutzten Palast nur die konkav geschwungene Toranlage mit dem doppelsäulenflankierten Portal und die Eckpavillons übrig. Das nun als Herzstück des PalaisQuartiers in verkleinertem Maßstab rekonstruierte Gebäude wird gewerblich genutzt.

THURN & TAXIS PALACE *Prince Anselm Franz von Thurn und Taxis had the most important imperial post office in the Old Empire constructed in the form of a late baroque three-wing complex. The palace was used as the seat of the German federal assembly from 1816-1866. After the horrific destruction during the war, the only part of it that had survived was the concave curved gate complex including the portal framed by pairs of columns and the corner pavilions. The building that has now been reconstructed on a smaller scale as the heart of the PalaisQuartier development project is used for commercial purposes.*

Adresse: Thurn-und-Taxis-Platz 1 | **Stadtteil:** Innenstadt | **Erbauung:** 1731–1741; Rekonstruktion: 2004–2009 | **Architekten:** Robert de Cotte, Guillaume d'Hauberat; Architekturbüro KSP Engel und Zimmermann (Rekonstruktion)

Die Familie Goethe fasste zwei in ihrem Besitz befindliche Fachwerkhäuser, in deren kleinerem Johann Wolfgang 1749 zur Welt gekommen war, sechs Jahre später zu einem spätbarocken Bürgerhaus zusammen. Das steinerne Erdgeschoss sowie die darüberliegenden Fachwerkgeschosse wurden verputzt. Seit 1863 ist das Gebäude im Besitz des Freien Deutschen Hochstifts und dient als Gedenkstätte. Im Krieg komplett ruiniert, wurde es anschließend originalgetreu rekonstruiert und ist heute Museum.

GOETHE HOUSE

The Goethe family owned two half-timbered houses, and little Johann

Goethehaus | 26

Wolfgang was born in the smaller of the two in 1749. Six years later the family combined the two buildings to create a late baroque burgher's residence. The stone ground floor as well as the half-timbered levels above were finished with stucco. Since 1863 the building has been owned by a foundation - "Freier Deutscher Hochstift" - and has served as a memorial site. During the war it was completely destroyed. Afterwards, it was restored to its original condition to as great an extent as possible, and today it is a museum.

Adresse: Großer Hirschgraben 23
Stadtteil: Innenstadt
Erbauung: 1755–1756; Wiederaufbau: 1947–1951

27 | Bolongaropalast

Als Teil der vom Mainzer Kurfürsten Emmerich Joseph geplanten Höchster Neustadt ließ das italienische Brüderpaar Bolongaro, das durch die Herstellung und den Verkauf von Tabak reich geworden war, die spätbarocke hufeisenförmige Anlage errichten. Der Hauptflügel des schlossartigen Baus erstreckt sich auf 117 Metern und wartet im Inneren mit beeindruckenden Prunkräumen auf. Besonders reizvoll ist der terrassenförmig angelegte Garten mit seinen beiden Pavillons.

BOLONGARO PALACE *The Italian Bolongaro brothers, who had become wealthy through the manufacture and sale of tobacco, had the late baroque, horseshoe-shaped complex built as part of the "Neustadt" (new town) of Höchst planned by Elector Emmerich Joseph of Mainz. The main wing of the castle-like structure is 117 metres long, and the interior offers impressive showcase rooms. The garden with its two pavilions, which is laid out in terrace form, is particularly lovely.*

Adresse: Bolongarostraße 109 | **Stadtteil:** Höchst | **Erbauung:** 1772–1780
Architekt: vermutlich Jakob Joseph Schneider

Haus Zum Paradies und Grimmvogel | 28

Das heutige Eckhaus mit seinen symmetrisch gestalteten Fassaden lässt nicht mehr erahnen, dass hier ursprünglich zwei sehr unterschiedliche mittelalterliche Gebäude standen. Nur in den Dachgiebeln findet man darauf Hinweise, nämlich das Wappen des früheren Besitzers Siegfried zum Paradies (Richtung Liebfrauenberg) und den Grimm-, also Raubvogel (Richtung Neue Kräme). Das spätbarocke Bürgerpalais musste im Zweiten Weltkrieg nur die Zerstörung des Dachbereichs verkraften.

Zum Paradies & Grimmvogel House *The present corner building with its symmetrically designed façades give no sign that there were originally two very different medieval buildings at this location. The only traces can be found in the roof gables, namely the coat of arms of the former owner Siegfried zum Paradies (side facing Liebfrauenberg) and the "Grimmvogel", i.e. bird of prey (side facing Neue Kräme). During the Second World War, the only part of the late baroque burgher's palace that was destroyed was the roof section.*

Adresse: Liebfrauenberg 39 / Neue Kräme 34 | **Stadtteil:** Altstadt | **Erbauung:** 1775
Architekt: Johann Wilhelm Kayser

29 | Paulskirche

Die Revolutionskriege waren dafür verantwortlich, dass die Arbeiten an dem klassizistischen Gebäude nur langsam vorankamen und drei Stadtbaumeister verschlissen. Der Zentralbau auf ovalem Grundriss wurde evangelische Hauptkirche der Stadt und war 1848–1849 Tagungsort der ersten deutschen Nationalversammlung. Wegen ihrer großen symbolischen Bedeutung wurde die Paulskirche nach der Kriegszerstörung sofort wieder aufgebaut, wobei das Innere allerdings modern verändert wurde.

CHURCH OF ST. PAUL *The revolutionary wars were responsible for slowing down the work on the classicistic building so that the project went through three city master builders. The central structure with an oval layout became the main Protestant church of the city and from 1848 -1849 it was the venue used for the first German national assembly. Because of its great symbolic importance, it was rebuilt immediately after it was destroyed during the war. However, the interior was altered and finished in a more modern vein.*

Adresse: Paulsplatz 11 | **Stadtteil:** Altstadt | **Erbauung:** 1789–1833; Wiederaufbau: 1947–1948
Architekten: Johann Andreas Liebhardt, Johann Friedrich Georg Hess, Johann Friedrich Christian Hess; Rudolf Schwarz (Wiederaufbau)

Alte Stadtbibliothek | 30

„Nach zurückgewonnener Freiheit [weiht] die Stadt [dieses Gebäude] den Wissenschaften“, verkündet die von Arthur Schopenhauer entworfene lateinische Giebelinschrift des klassizistischen Bauwerks, von dem der Zweite Weltkrieg nur den Säulenvorbau übrig ließ. 1987–2003 befand sich im dahinter aufgestellten Container der innovative Ausstellungsraum „Portikus“. Der Wiederaufbau erfolgte auf der Basis privater Finanzierung durch Frankfurter Bürger, Stiftungen und Institutionen.

Old City Library *After the Second World War only the portico of this classicistic building had survived: the Latin inscription on the gable was designed by Arthur Schopenhauer and proclaims "After freedom is regained the city dedicates this building to the sciences". From 1987-2003 a container that was set up behind the portico housed the innovative "Portikus" exhibition hall. The reconstruction was financed privately using funds donated by Frankfurt's citizens, foundations and institutions.*

Adresse: Schöne Aussicht 2 | **Stadtteil:** Innenstadt
Erbauung: 1820–1825; Rekonstruktion: 2003–2005
Architekten: Johann Friedrich Christian Hess; Christoph Mäckler (Rekonstruktion)

31 | Hauptfriedhof – Altes Portal und Trauerhalle

Der Hauptfriedhof löste 1828 den Peterskirchhof als zentrale Begräbnisstätte Frankfurts ab. Den ältesten Teil betritt man durch einen antikisierenden Portalbau mit monumentalen dorischen Säulen, an den sich seitlich zwei symmetrische Flügelbauten anschließen, die ursprünglich als Leichenhaus und Kapelle dienten. Die Trauerhalle, ein eindrucksvoll gestaffelter Gebäudekomplex aus Vorhalle, Kuppelkirche und Leichenhalle, ist vorwiegend in neoklassizistischen Formen gestaltet.

MAIN CEMETERY – OLD GATE AND CHAPEL *In 1828 the Main Cemetery replaced St. Peter's Churchyard as the central burial site for Frankfurt. The entrance to the oldest section is through a portal structure in the classical style with monumental Doric columns. It is framed on both sides by two symmetrical wings that originally served as the mortuary and the chapel. The chapel, which is an impressively staggered complex of buildings consisting of an anteroom, a domed hall and a mortuary hall, was designed using neo-classicistic elements.*

Adresse: Eckenheimer Ldstr. 188–190 (Altes Portal); Eckenheimer Ldstr. 194–196 (Trauerhalle)
Stadtteil: Nordend | **Erbauung:** 1826–1828 (Altes Portal); 1909 (Trauerhalle)
Architekten: Friedrich Rumpf (Altes Portal); Heinrich Reinhardt, Georg Süßenguth (Trauerhalle)

Burnitzbau | 32

Für das nach seinem Architekten benannte Gebäude wurde der Eckturm der staufischen Burg niedergelegt. Der viergeschossige Wohnbau mit acht Fensterachsen verlässt erstmals den in Frankfurt seit Anfang des 19. Jhs. vorherrschenden strengen Klassizismus und entwickelt ihn ins Romantische weiter. Stilelemente aus der Romanik wie Rundfenster und Zinnenkranz erinnern an mittelalterliche Paläste und stellen einen Kontext zum benachbarten Saalhof her.

BURNITZ BUILDING *The corner tower of the castle from the Staufer period was torn down for this building, which bears the name of the architect. The four-storey residential building with eight window axes is the first building to abandon the severe Classicism that had predominated in Frankfurt since the beginning of the 19th century and move on towards the romantic style. Stylistic elements from the Romanesque period such as rounded windows and crenellation are reminiscent of medieval palaces and thus create a contextual reference to the neighbouring "Saalhof".*

Adresse: Mainkai | **Stadtteil:** Altstadt | **Erbauung:** 1842–1843
Architekt: Rudolf Burnitz

33 | Eiserner Steg

1867 gründeten Frankfurter Bürger die „Aktiengesellschaft zur Errichtung einer Eisernen Brücke am Fahrtor". Die Nutzung der in innovativer Eisenfachwerktechnik errichteten Hängebrücke mit ihren Strompfeilern und Brückenköpfen aus Sandstein war für die Fußgänger so lange gebührenpflichtig, bis sie sich amortisiert hatte (im Jahr 1884). Die ursprünglichen neugotischen Fialen oberhalb der Pfeiler wurden bei Umbauarbeiten entfernt.

IRON FOOTBRIDGE *In 1867 the citizens of Frankfurt founded a joint stock company for the construction of an iron bridge at the Fahrtor location: "Aktiengesellschaft zur Errichtung einer Eisernen Brücke am Fahrtor". Until the bridge had paid for itself (in the year 1884), pedestrians had to pay a fee for using the suspension bridge. Its piers and bridge heads are made of sandstone, and it was erected using innovative specialised ironwork technology. The original Neo-Gothic pinnacles above the piers were removed during alteration work.*

Adresse: Mainkai / Schaumainkai | **Stadtteil:** Altstadt / Sachsenhausen
Erbauung: 1868–1869 | **Architekt:** Johann Peter Wilhelm Schmick

Palmengarten-Gesellschaftshaus | 34

Nach dem Kauf der Sammlung exotischer Pflanzen des Herzogs Adolph von Nassau wurde für ihre Ausstellung der Palmengarten angelegt. Das erste von Kaysser errichtete Gesellschaftshaus brannte ab und wurde durch den Neorenaissance-Bau von Schmidt ersetzt. Im Stil der klassischen Moderne umgebaut und nach Kriegsbeschädigungen vereinfacht wieder aufgebaut und erweitert, wobei auch der Festsaal („Frankfurts Bernsteinzimmer“) stark verändert wurde, wird dieser nun rekonstruiert.

PALMENGARTEN RECEPTION HALL *After Duke Adolph von Nassau's collection of exotic plants was purchased, the "Palmengarten" botanical garden was created to house the exhibition. The first reception hall building built by Kaysser burned down and was replaced by the Neo-Renaissance building designed by Schmidt. That building was altered in the classic modern style. After the damage incurred during the war, it was rebuilt and enlarged in a more austere style whereby the ballroom ("Frankfurt's Amber Room") was changed radically. Now the latter is being reconstructed.*

Adresse: Siesmayerstraße 61 | **Stadtteil:** Westend | **Erbauung:** 1869–1871; Neubau: 1879; Umbau: 1928–1929; Sanierung und Anbau: 2009–2011 | **Architekten:** F. Kaysser; H. T. Schmidt (Neubau); E. May, M. Elsaesser, W. Hebebrand (Umbau); D. Chipperfield (Sanierung und Anbau)

35 | Alte Oper

Richard Lucae schuf Frankfurts Opernhaus als Repräsentationsbau der Neorenaissance in der Tradition Gottfried Sempers mit gestufter Hauptfront und aufwendigem Skulpturenschmuck aus französischem Kalkstein. Das im Zweiten Weltkrieg zerstörte und völlig ausgebrannte Gebäude wurde rekonstruiert, wobei es im Inneren größtenteils modern ausgebaut wurde, um den heutigen Anforderungen eines Konzert- und Kongresszentrums genügen zu können.

OLD OPERA HOUSE *Richard Lucae created Frankfurt's opera house as a prestigious Neo-Renaissance structure in the tradition of Gottfried Semper, with a stepped main façade and intricate, decorative sculptural details made of French limestone. The building was destroyed and completely gutted by fire during World War II. It was reconstructed, whereby most of the interior was finished in the modern style in order to accommodate the present requirements placed on a concert and convention centre.*

Adresse: Opernplatz 1 | **Stadtteil:** Innenstadt
Erbauung: 1873–1880; Wiederaufbau: 1976–1981
Architekten: Richard Lucae; Helmut + W. Braun, Martin Schlockermann, I. Voigt (Wiederaufbau)

Frankfurter Hof | 36

Mit der Gründung der „Frankfurter Hotel-Actien-Gesellschaft" 1872 schlug die Geburtsstunde des Frankfurter Hofs. Das neue Grandhotel, bereits in Hinsicht auf den Bau des Zentralbahnhofs projektiert, entstand als Dreiflügelanlage auf H-förmigem Grundriss mit reich dekorierter Fassade zum Kaiserplatz. Durch das Kriegsbombardement zerstörte Mansarddächer wurden durch einfachere ersetzt, in den 1950er Jahren erfolgte nach Süden eine formal entsprechende Erweiterung des Hauses.

FRANKFURTER HOF HOTEL *The foundation of the "Frankfurter Hotel-Actien-Gesellschaft", a hotel stock company, in 1872 was the hour of birth of the Frankfurter Hof. The new "grand hotel", which was already designed with a view to the construction of the central train station, was erected as a three-wing complex with an H-shaped layout and an intricately decorated façade facing Kaiserplatz. The mansard roofs, which were destroyed by the bombing during the war, were replaced in a simpler style. In the fifties an addition in the style of the older building was built on the south side of the building.*

Adresse: Am Kaiserplatz | **Stadtteil:** Innenstadt | **Erbauung:** 1874–1876
Architekten: Carl Jonas Mylius, Friedrich Albert Bluntschli

37 | Städelsches Kunstinstitut

Das nach seinem Stifter, dem Kunstsammler Johann Friedrich Städel, benannte Museum erhielt einen imposanten Neubau im Stil der Neorenaissance mit einem durch Freitreppe, Doppelsäulen und Zentralkuppel betonten Mittelrisalit. Die kriegszerstörten Eckpavillons ersetzte Krahn betont schlicht. Der durch eine Brücke verbundene Erweiterungsbau entlang der Holbeinstraße respektiert in seinen Maßen das alte „Städel", zeigt aber trotzdem deutlich seine Eigenständigkeit.

STÄDEL MUSEUM OF ART *The museum was named after its founder, the art collector Johann Friedrich Städel. An imposing new building in the Neo-Renaissance style was built to accommodate it, with a central projection that is accentuated by an outside staircase, pairs of columns and a central dome. Krahn replaced the corner pavilions that were destroyed during the war with purposely austere elements. The addition along Holbeinstraße, which is connected by a bridge, shows respect for the old "Städel" in its dimensions, but nevertheless, it clearly demonstrates its independence.*

Adresse: Schaumainkai 63 | **Stadtteil:** Sachsenhausen
Erbauung: 1874–1878; Wiederaufbau: 1959–1963; Erweiterungsbau: 1988–1990
Architekten: Oskar Sommer; Johannes Krahn (Wiederaufbau); Gustav Peichl (Erweiterungsbau)

Börse | 38

Das monumentale Gebäude im Stil der Neorenaissance wirkt sehr repräsentativ mit der großzügigen Vorhalle, den Doppelsäulen, den rustifizierten Eckrisaliten, dem Zyklus allegorischer Figuren und dem gewaltigen, 43 Meter hohen Kuppeldach. Die Architekten bedienen sich einer ähnlichen Formensprache wie beim Städelschen Kunstinstitut, das sie ebenfalls entworfen haben. Das ausgebrannte Innere wurde in den 1950er Jahren modern gestaltet.

STOCK EXCHANGE *The monumental building in the Neo-Renaissance style makes a very prestigious impression with its spacious anteroom, pairs of columns, corner projections in the rustic style, a cycle of allegorical figures and its huge 43 metre high domed roof. The architects used similar stylistic elements here as in the Städel Museum of Art, which they also designed. The interior, which was gutted by fire, was redesigned in the modern style in the fifties.*

Adresse: Börsenplatz 2–6 | **Stadtteil:** Innenstadt | **Erbauung:** 1874–1879
Architekten: Heinrich Burnitz, Oskar Sommer

39 | Gutleutkaserne

Heute steht von der ehemaligen preußischen Infanteriekaserne nur noch der denkmalgeschützte Kopfbau. Ursprünglich handelte es sich um ein Geviert von 260 x 170 Metern Länge. Der lang gestreckte Klinkerbau ist durch Türme rhythmisiert und in Zwischenbauten gegliedert sowie mit neoromanischer Bauplastik aus rotem Sandstein dekoriert. Die Architektur erinnert an lombardische Burgen und entsprach seinerzeit dem standardisierten preußischen Bauschema für Militärbauten.

GUTLEUT BARRACKS *Today the only part of the former Prussian infantry barracks that still exists is the front section, which is a protected historical landmark. Originally, the complex was a rectangle measuring 260 x 170 metres. The elongate brick structure is rhythmically accentuated with towers and divided into connecting sections. It is also decorated with Neo-Romanesque architectural sculpture made of red sandstone. The architecture is reminiscent of Lombardian castles: at the time it was in line with the standardised Prussian building concept for military structures.*

Adresse: Gutleutstraße 112–116 | **Stadtteil:** Gutleutviertel | **Erbauung:** 1877–1879
Architekten: F. Bruhn und A. C. Zacharias

Hauptbahnhof | 40

Die bei der Einweihung größte Eisenbahnstation des Kontinents verfügt über ein dreiflügeliges symmetrisches Empfangsgebäude aus gelbem Sandstein im Neorenaissance-Stil. Die gesamte Fassade ist mit einem allegorischen Skulpturenprogramm zum Thema Handel und Verkehr geschmückt, das in der Atlantengruppe auf dem Dach gipfelt. Wegen der Zunahme des Zugverkehrs mussten den ursprünglichen drei Gleishallen schon bald zwei weitere angegliedert werden.

MAIN RAILWAY STATION *When it was officially opened the railway station was the largest on the continent. The symmetrical three-wing reception building was built of yellow sandstone in the Neo-Renaissance style. The entire façade is decorated with a series of allegorical sculptural elements on the trade and transportation theme, which culminates in the Atlas group on the roof. The three original platform halls had to be enlarged by two additional halls because of the increase in rail traffic.*

Adresse: Am Hauptbahnhof | **Stadtteil:** Gallusviertel
Erbauung: 1883–1888; Erweiterungsbau: 1912–1924
Architekten: Hermann Eggert (Empfangsgebäude), Johann Wilhelm Schwedler (Gleishalle)

41 | Bockenheimer Depot

Kernstück des ehemaligen Straßenbahndepots ist die dreischiffige Halle aus unverputztem gelbem Ziegelmauerwerk mit roten Gesimsen und Zierbändern. Die Giebelseite ist durch Pfeiler gegliedert und weist ein halbrundes Fenster auf. Bemerkenswert ist die hölzerne Dachkonstruktion aus halbkreisförmigen Bogenbindern, die auf den französischen Renaissance-Baumeister Philibert Delorme zurückgeht. Seit dem Umbau ist die denkmalgeschützte Halle Spielstätte der Städtischen Bühnen Frankfurt.

BOCKENHEIMER DEPOT *The heart of the former streetcar depot is the three-bay hall made of unfinished yellow brick masonry with red cornices and decorative strips. The gable side is divided by pillars and has a semicircular window. The wooden roof structure made of semicircular curved cross-beams, which is based on a design by the French Renaissance master builder Philibert Delorme, is particularly worthy of note.*
The hall is a protected historical landmark. Since the conversion it has served as the theatre venue for the Städtische Bühnen Frankfurt ensemble.

Adresse: Carlo-Schmid-Platz 1 | **Stadtteil:** Bockenheim | **Erbauung:** 1899; Umbau: 1988
Architekten: Klaus Peter Heinrici, Klaus-Georg Geiger (Umbau)

Altes Rathaus | 42

Für die Erweiterung des Rathauses Römer mussten mehrere Altstadtgebäude weichen. Nördlich und südlich der neu trassierten Bethmannstraße entstanden zwei monumentale Baukomplexe in unterschiedlichen historisierenden Stilen, die durch eine Bogenbrücke („Beamtenlaufbahn") miteinander verbunden sind. Die aufwendige Fassadendekoration illustriert das städtische Gemeinwesen in allegorischer Weise und durch Verkörperungen berühmter Frankfurter Persönlichkeiten.

OLD CITY HALL *Several buildings in the old medieval centre had to be torn down to make room for the enlargement of the Römer city hall. Two monumental building complexes using different historical styles that are connected by an arched bridge nicknamed "Beamtenlaufbahn" (i.e. civil servant's career path) were built on the north and south sides of Bethmannstraße, the roadway of which was moved to a new location. The intricate façade decoration illustrates the urban community with allegorical elements and with representations of famous Frankfurt public figures.*

Adresse: Paulsplatz 5–9 | **Stadtteil:** Altstadt | **Erbauung:** 1900–1908
Architekten: Franz von Hoven, Ludwig Neher

43 | Senckenberg – Forschungsinstitut und Naturmuseum

Das Institut wurde in der späten Gründerzeit für die „Senckenbergische naturforschende Gesellschaft“ in der Tradition des barocken Schlossbaus aus Mainsandstein errichtet. Die repräsentative Front zeichnet sich durch einen figurenverzierten Giebel aus und wird von Saturn mit Sanduhr und Sense bekrönt. Offene Arkaden schaffen eine Verbindung zu den Flügelbauten des „Physikalischen Vereins“ und der „Senckenbergischen Bibliothek“.

RESEARCH INSTITUTE AND NATURAL SCIENCE MUSEUM *The institute was built for the "Senckenbergische naturforschende Gesellschaft" (Senckenberg Society for Natural Science Research) in the late Wilhelminian period, in the tradition of baroque castle construction and using Main sandstone. The prestigious front façade is accentuated by a gable decorated with figures and crowned by Saturn holding an hourglass and a scythe. Open arcades serve to connect the wing sections of the "Physikalischer Verein" (Physics Association) and the library - "Senckenbergische Bibliothek".*

Adresse: Senckenberganlage 25 | **Stadtteil:** Westend | **Erbauung:** 1904–1907
Architekt: Ludwig Neher

Jügelhaus der Goethe-Universität | 44

Das neobarocke Gebäude wurde im Zusammenhang mit dem sich südlich anschließenden Senckenbergischen Baukomplex als „Akademie für Handels- und Sozialwissenschaften" vom selben Architekten entworfen. Die Ähnlichkeit der Handschrift ist erkennbar, wobei sich die Sandsteinfassade des Jügelhauses formal an den Mittelbau des Mannheimer Schlosses anlehnt. Nach den Zerstörungen des Zweiten Weltkrieges wurde es, insbesondere im Inneren, stark verändert.

Jügel Building of the Goethe University *The Neo-Baroque building was designed by the same architect as an "academy for commercial and social sciences" in conjunction with the Senckenberg building complex, which is situated immediately adjacent to the south. The similarity of the design is obvious, whereby the sandstone façade of the Jügel Building is formally modelled after the central section of Mannheim Castle. After the destruction of World War II it was altered radically, especially on the inside.*

Adresse: Mertonstraße 17–21 | **Stadtteil:** Westend | **Erbauung:** 1906; Wiederaufbau: 1953
Architekten: Ludwig Neher; Ferdinand Kramer (Wiederaufbau)

45 | Festhalle

Auf einem an den Längsseiten gerundeten Rechteck von 115 x 45 Metern sitzt zwischen steinernen Ecktürmen in über 30 Metern Höhe die imposante Kuppel. Die eiserne Tragkonstruktion kommt dabei ohne Mittelstützen aus, da die Streben an einem Sprengring von 18,5 Metern Durchmesser zusammentreffen. Die Festhalle, Anfang des 20. Jhs. der größte Hallenbau Europas, wird heute für Ausstellungen sowie kulturelle und sportliche Veranstaltungen genutzt.

FESTIVAL HALL *The imposing dome at a height of 30 metres rests between stone corner towers on a rectangular base with rounded longitudinal sides measuring 115 x 45 metres. The iron supporting structure dispenses with central supports, because the trusses are connected to an anchoring structural collar with a diameter of 18.5 metres. At the beginning of the 20th century the Festival Hall was the largest hall structure in Europe. Today it is used for exhibitions as well as for cultural and sports events.*

Adresse: Ludwig-Erhard-Anlage 1 | **Stadtteil:** Westend | **Erbauung:** 1907–1909
Architekt: Friedrich Max Ritter von Thiersch

Westendsynagoge | 46

Die Westendsynagoge ist das geistliche Zentrum der jüdischen Gemeinde Frankfurts. Sie liegt hinter einem Vorhof und ist ein neoklassizistischer Kuppelbau aus Muschelkalk mit orientalischen Anmutungen. Schwer beschädigt durch die Reichspogromnacht und den Zweiten Weltkrieg, wurde sie nach provisorischer Renovierung wiedereingeweiht. Vier Jahrzehnte später legte man die Reste der alten Innenausstattung frei und rekonstruierte sie auf dieser Basis wieder originalgetreu.

WESTEND SYNAGOGUE *The Westend Synagogue is the spiritual centre of the Jewish community in Frankfurt. It is situated behind a front courtyard. It is a neo-classicistic domed structure made of shell limestone that makes an oriental impression. It was severely damaged during the Night of Broken Glass and World War II, but it was reconsecrated after a provisional renovation. Four decades later the remains of the old interior decoration have been uncovered and used as the basis to restore the synagogue to the original to as great an extent as possible.*

Adresse: Freiherr-vom-Stein-Straße 30 | **Stadtteil:** Westend | **Erbauung:** 1908–1910; 1948–1950 (Wiederaufbau); 1988–1992 (Rekonstruktion) | **Architekten:** Franz Roeckle; Max Kemper, Werner Hebebrand, Hans Leistikow (Wiederaufbau); Hendryk Isenberg (Rekonstruktion)

47 | Honsellbrücke

Frankfurts einzige Jugendstilbrücke bildet den Auftakt zum 1912 eingeweihten Osthafen. Sie überspannt die Einfahrt zu den beiden Becken des Unterhafens, blieb allerdings Torso einer ursprünglich zweiteilig geplanten Anlage, die bis zum Sachsenhäuser Ufer reichen sollte. Durch ihre Sichelbogenform wirkt sie fast schwerelos. Basaltbrüstung, Bauplastik (Panther, Lastträger) und Straßenlaternen sind noch original erhalten und stehen unter Denkmalschutz.

HONSELL BRIDGE *Frankfurt's only Art Nouveau bridge marks the entrance to the "Osthafen", the eastern harbour facility that was officially opened in 1912. It arches over the entrance to the two basins of the lower harbour. However, the originally planned complex consisting of two sections, which was supposed to go as far as the Sachsenshausen riverbank, remained unfinished. The sickle-shape of the arches makes it appear almost weightless. The original basalt balustrade, architectural sculptures (panther, load carriers) and street lamps have survived and are protected as a historic landmark.*

Adresse: Honsellstraße / Franziusstraße | **Stadtteil:** Ostend | **Erbauung:** 1910–1911
Architekt: Städtisches Tiefbauamt

Peter-Behrens-Bau | 48

Der Verwaltungsbau aus rotem und violettem Backstein gehört zu den wichtigsten Beispielen expressionistischer Architektur in Deutschland. Die beiden lang gestreckten Büroflügel werden von einem markanten Mittelbau mit Turm und Brücke akzentuiert, der in stilisierter Form als Firmenlogo der Hoechst AG (1947–1997) weltbekannt wurde. Im Inneren ist vor allen Dingen die große Halle mit ihren stalaktitförmigen farbig gefassten Pfeilern und den Glaskuppeln sehenswert.

PETER BEHRENS BUILDING *The administrative building built of red and purple brick is one of the most important examples of expressionistic architecture in Germany. The two elongate office wings are accentuated by a striking central section with a tower and bridge, which attained worldwide fame in stylised form as the corporate logo of the Hoechst AG (1947-1997). Inside the large hall with its stalactite-shaped, colour accented pillars and glass domes is particularly well worth a visit.*

Adresse: Brüningstraße, Gebäude C 770 | **Stadtteil:** Höchst (Industriepark Höchst)
Erbauung: 1920–1924 | **Architekt:** Peter Behrens

49 | Mousonturm

Als die 1798 gegründete Seifen- und Parfümfabrik Mouson eine Erweiterung benötigte, entwarf der damalige Juniorchef Fritz Mouson aus Platzmangel das mit einer Höhe von 33 Metern erste Hochhaus Frankfurts. Nach dem Verkauf des Unternehmens 1972 wurden alle Gebäude bis auf den expressionistischen Industriebau mit seiner abwechslungsreichen Klinkerfassade abgerissen. Der denkmalgeschützte Mousonturm ist seit 1988 Spiel- und Produktionsstätte für freischaffende Künstler.

MOUSON TOWER *When the Mouson soap and perfume factory - which was founded in 1798 - needed to be enlarged, because of space constraints Fritz Mouson, who was at that time the junior partner, designed the first high-rise building in Frankfurt, which was 33 metres tall. After the company was sold in 1972, all of the buildings were torn down - with the exception of this expressionistic industrial structure with its variegated clinker brick façade. The "Mousonturm" is a protected historic landmark. Since 1988 it has been a performance and production venue for freelance artists.*

Adresse: Waldschmidtstraße 4 | **Stadtteil:** Ostend | **Erbauung:** 1924–1926
Architekt: Fritz Mouson

Alte Brücke | 50

Die älteste Mainbrücke Frankfurts wird zwar 1222 erstmals urkundlich erwähnt, geht aber in ihrer heutigen Gestalt auf das 20. Jh. zurück. Im Gegensatz zu ihrer Vorgängerin wurde sie nach dem Ersten Weltkrieg formal vereinfacht, in der Bogenzahl reduziert und als mit Sandstein verkleideter Betonbau ausgeführt. Nach dem Zweiten Weltkrieg wurde das lang gestreckte Mittelstück eingefügt, um dem Schiffsverkehr die Durchfahrt zu erleichtern.

Old Bridge *The first documentary evidence of the oldest bridge over the Main in Frankfurt is from 1222, but its present appearance originated in the 20th century. Unlike its predecessor, after World War I it was formally simplified: the number of arches was reduced and it was erected in the form of a concrete structure sheathed with sandstone. After World War II, the elongate central section was inserted in order to facilitate the passage of shipping traffic.*

Adresse: Mainkai, Schöne Aussicht / Sachsenhäuser Ufer | **Stadtteil:** Altstadt / Sachsenhausen
Erbauung: 1914–1926; 1965 (Umbau)
Architekten: Hermann von Hoven junior, Franz Heberer, Carl Friedrich Wilhelm Leonhardt

51 | St. Bonifatius

Die Klinkerfassade von St. Bonifatius, die wie eine expressionistische Variante der norddeutschen Backsteingotik wirkt, verbrämt die darunterliegende Eisenbetonkonstruktion. Höhepunkte der damals in Frankfurt außergewöhnlichen Sakralarchitektur sind die großzügige Freitreppe und der genau gegenüberliegende hexagonale Turm, von dem vier Seiten zugleich den Chorabschluss bilden. Seit 2005 ist hier neben der Gemeinde auch die katholische Jugendkirche JONA beheimatet.

ST. BONIFATIUS *St. Bonifatius looks like an expressionistic variation on the Northern German brick Gothic style. The clinker brick façade serves to conceal the reinforced concrete structure beneath. The highlights of this type of ecclesiastical architecture - which was quite unusual in Frankfurt at that time - are the generously proportioned outside staircase and the hexagonal tower directly opposite, the four sides of which delineate the choir. Since 2005 it has been used by JONA, the Roman Catholic youth congregation, as well as the local parish.*

Adresse: Holbeinstraße 70 | **Stadtteil:** Sachsenhausen | **Erbauung:** 1926–1927
Architekt: Martin Weber

Großmarkthalle | 52

Zu seiner Zeit war der verklinkerte Betonskelettbau mit den imposanten Maßen (220 Meter Länge, 50 Meter Breite, 23 Meter Höhe) die größte freitragende Halle Europas. Das enorme Raumvolumen sorgte für optimale Hygiene- und Lagerbedingungen aufgrund guter Durchlüftung und Kühlung. Die Dachkonstruktion aus nur sechs Zentimeter dünnen und damit leichten Betonschalen war ausgesprochen innovativ. Das denkmalgeschützte Anwesen wurde 2005 an die Europäische Zentralbank verkauft.

WHOLESALE MARKET HALL *In its time, this concrete frame building was the largest self-supporting hall in Europe. It is sheathed in clinker brick and its dimensions are truly impressive (220 metres in length, 50 metres wide, 23 metres high). The enormous volume of spaces ensured optimum hygiene and storage conditions thanks to good ventilation and cooling attributes. The roof structure was extremely innovative: it consists of concrete shells that are only six centimetres thick and thus quite light. The complex, which is a protected historical landmark, was sold to the European Central Bank in 2005.*

Adresse: Rückertstraße 2–6 | **Stadtteil:** Ostend | **Erbauung:** 1926–1928
Architekt: Martin Elsässer

53 | Ernst-May-Haus (Siedlung Römerstadt)

In seiner Zeit als Frankfurter Siedlungsdezernent (1925–1930) realisierte Ernst May eines der umfangreichsten und bedeutendsten Bauprogramme der Weimarer Republik mit etwa 15.000 Wohnungen zu erschwinglichen Preisen. Das „Neue Frankfurt" sollte jedem Bewohner ein Leben in Luft, Licht und Raum ermöglichen. Das restaurierte Reihenhaus mit seiner originalen „Frankfurter Küche" sowie dem rekonstruierten Nutz- und Ziergarten kann von Architekturinteressierten besichtigt werden.

Ernst May House – Römerstadt Housing Development *During his time as Frankfurt's housing development officer (1925-1930), Ernst May realised one of the most extensive and significant construction programmes of the Weimar Republic, thus creating about 15,000 apartments for affordable prices. The "New Frankfurt" was supposed to make it possible for every resident to live with air, light and space. People interested in architecture can tour the restored row house with its original "Frankfurt kitchen" along with the reconstructed fruit and vegetable garden as well as a flower garden.*

Adresse: Im Burgfeld 136 | **Stadtteil:** Heddernheim | **Erbauung:** 1928
Architekten: Ernst May, Herbert Boehm, Wolfgang Bangert

IG Farben-Haus | 54

Das IG Farben-Haus galt als größter Verwaltungsbau seiner Zeit und blieb bis in die 1950er Jahre das modernste Bürohaus Europas. Um es trotz seiner 250 Meter Länge nicht zu wuchtig erscheinen zu lassen, entwarf Poelzig einen segmentbogenförmigen Hauptflügel mit sechs radial angeordneten Querflügeln. Wie das seitlich angeschlossene Labor- und das separate Casinogebäude ist es mit Travertinplatten verkleidet. Heute bildet der Komplex den Kern des Campus Westend der Goethe-Universität.

IG FARBEN BUILDING *The IG Farben Building was said to be the largest administrative building of its time, and until the fifties it was the most modern office building in Europe. To ensure that it did not appear too massive in spite of its 250 metres length, Poelzig designed a main wing in the shape of an arc segment with six transverse wings that are positioned radially. It is sheathed in travertine slabs just like the adjoining laboratory on the side and the separate cafeteria building. Today the complex forms the core of the Westend Campus of the Goethe University.*

Adresse: Grüneburgplatz 1 | **Stadtteil:** Westend | **Erbauung:** 1929–1931; Umbau: 1998–2001
Architekten: Hans Poelzig; Architekturbüro Dissing + Weitling, Dänemark (Umbau)

55 | Juniorhaus

Das die Ecke Kaiserstraße / Friedenstraße mit seinem runden glasverkleideten Treppenhaus betonende Gebäude gehört zu den bedeutenden Leistungen des Wiederaufbaus der Frankfurter Innenstadt. Der Architekt nimmt sowohl die nachbarschaftliche Situation der gründerzeitlichen Bebauung auf als auch die Ideen des neuen Bauens der Vorkriegszeit. Die Natursteinfassade wie die Messingprofile des Treppenhauses und der Fenster wurden anfangs für die Zeit als zu luxuriös kritisiert.

JUNIOR BUILDING *The building that accentuates the corner of Kaiserstraße & Friedenstraße with its round, glass-sheathed stairway is one of the most important achievements of the reconstruction of Frankfurt's city centre. The architect has incorporated the character of the surrounding Wilhelminian buildings as well as the concepts of the new building style of the pre-War era. In the beginning, the natural stone façade as well as the brass profiles in the stairway and the windows were criticised as being too luxurious for the time.*

Adresse: Kaiserstraße 19-21 | **Stadtteil:** Innenstadt | **Erbauung:** 1951
Architekt: Wilhelm Berenzten

Bayerhaus | 56

Das heute als Hotel genutzte ursprüngliche Bürogebäude der Chemiefirma Bayer gehört zu den frühen Nachkriegshochhäusern Frankfurts. Das durch filigrane Säulen aufgeständerte Dach verleiht dem mit Naturstein verkleideten Bau seine Wirkung. Eine besondere Sehenswürdigkeit ist das luxuriöse Treppenhaus, das die gesamte Höhe des Gebäudes einnimmt. Hier fahren die in Frankfurt selten gewordenen Paternosteraufzüge.

BAYER BUILDING *The building was originally an office building belonging to the Bayer chemical company, and is now used as a hotel. It is one of Frankfurt's early post-war high-rise buildings. The structure sheathed in natural stone achieves its effect through the delicate columns supporting the roof. The luxurious stairway soaring the entire height of the building is a special point of interest. The paternoster elevators – which have become quite rare in Frankfurt – are still in operation.*

Adresse: Eschenheimer Tor 2 | **Stadtteil:** Innenstadt | **Erbauung:** 1952
Architekt: Stefan Blattner

57 | Olivetti-Häuser

Die trichterartigen Hochbauten in der Bürostadt Niederrad gehören zu den letzten Arbeiten Eiermanns. Der Architekt entwirft die für seine Häuser typischen arkadenartigen Umläufe. Diese sollen mit den vorgehängten weißen Sonnensegeln sowohl den Wärmeeintrag reduzieren als auch die Fassaden auflockern. Eiermann hatte für Frankfurt ebenfalls die Neckermann-Versandhauszentrale und ein nicht mehr bestehendes Bürohochhaus für Hoch-Tief entworfen.

OLIVETTI BUILDINGS *The funnel-shaped high-rise buildings in the office district of Niederrad are among the last works of the architect. Eiermann's design includes the typical circular arcade-like walkways that are so typical of his buildings. Together with the curtain-type white awnings they are aimed at reducing heat input as well as at livening up the façades. In Frankfurt Eiermann also designed the head office of the Neckermann mail order company and a high-rise office building for Hoch-Tief that no longer exists.*

Adresse: Lyoner Straße 10 | **Stadtteil:** Niederrad | **Erbauung:** 1968–1972
Architekt: Egon Eiermann

Mit 337,50 Meter ist er einer der zwei höchsten Türme Deutschlands und gehört zu den höchsten in Europa. Er verjüngt sich von 20 Meter am Fuß auf 11 Meter unterhalb der Kanzel (218 Meter). Die Kanzel hat einen Durchmesser von 57 Meter. Auf dieser wie auch auf den sieben Plattformen darüber sind Parabolantennen für die Richtfunkstrecken der Deutschen Telekom installiert. Der Turm übernimmt seit 2004 auch die digitale Fernsehversorgung Frankfurts.

TELECOMMUNICATIONS TOWER

The structure is 337.50 metres high with a pulpit at a height of 218 metres, and is thus one of the two highest towers in Germany and one of the highest in

Fernmeldeturm | 58

Europe. The tower tapers from 20 metres at the base to 11 metres right below the pulpit, which has a diameter of 57 metres. Parabolic antennas for the radio relay system of Deutsche Telekom are installed on the pulpit as well as on the seven platforms. Since 2004 the tower has been supplying digital TV signals for Frankfurt.

Adresse: Wilhelm-Epstein-Straße
Stadtteil: Ginnheim
Erbauung: 1976–1978
Architekten: Johannes Möhrle, Peter Metzger und Erwin Heinle

59 | Europäische Zentralbank

Das ursprünglich für die Bank für Gemeinwirtschaft erbaute 143 Meter hohe Gebäude erhebt sich aus einem die Blockrandbebauung der Nachbarschaft aufnehmenden Sockel. Das prismenförmige Gebäude mit seiner aus Naturstein und Aluminium / Glas gestalteten Fassade wirkt von Süden schlank, von Westen breit in die Stadt gestellt. Seit 1994 ist es Sitz der Europäischen Zentralbank.

EUROPEAN CENTRAL BANK *The building was originally built for the Bank für Gemeinwirtschaft. It thrusts upwards from a plinth that reflects the perimeter block development of the immediate vicinity to a height of 143 metres. From the south, the prism-shaped building with a façade using natural stone and aluminium & glas appears slender, whereas from the west it presents a broad face to the city. It has been the domicile of the European Central Bank since 1994.*

Adresse: Kaiserstraße 29 | **Stadtteil:** Innenstadt | **Erbauung:** 1977
Architekten: Richard Heil, Johannes Krahn

Deutsche Bank | 60

Das 155 Meter hohe Gebäude steht wahrzeichenhaft für die Deutsche Bank, aber auch für Banken in Frankfurt. Die verspiegelten Doppeltürme wurden zunächst als Hotelbau konzipiert, aber bereits während des Baus für die Bank umgestaltet. Die Architektur der prismenartigen Gebäude ist ganz bewusst als Solitär ausgeführt. Durch die Renovierung 2009-2011 werden die Innenstruktur und Klimatechnik des Hauses deutlich verbessert.

DEUTSCHE BANK *The 155 metres high building is a veritable landmark that symbolises the Deutsche Bank, as well as the other banks in Frankfurt. The twin towers with their reflective façades were originally designed as a hotel building, but were already re-designed for the bank during the construction phase. The architectural concept of the prism-like buildings is purposely geared to the freestanding building complex. During the renovation 2009-2011 the interior structure as well as the air conditioning technology of the building will be improved substantially.*

Adresse: Taunusanlage 12 | **Stadtteil:** Innenstadt | **Erbauung:** 1979–1984, Renovierung 2009-2011 | **Architekten:** Walter Hanig, Heinz Scheid, Johannes Schmidt

Bis zur Fertigstellung des Messeturms 1990 war der „Silberturm" der Dresdner Bank mit 166 Metern Deutschlands höchstes Hochhaus. Das Gebäude mit seiner abgerundeten Aluminiumfassade steht auf einem System von Hartgummiballons, das automatisch die durch die Grundwasser-Veränderung mögliche Neigung des Büroturmes ausgleicht. Das Gebäude wird für die Nutzung der Deutschen Bahn renoviert.

DRESDNER BANK

Until the completion of the "Messeturm" - the tower on the trade fair grounds - in 1990, Dresdner Bank's "Silver Tower" with a height of 166 metres was the tallest building in Germany. The building with its curving aluminium façade rests on a system of hard rubber balloons that automatically compensate any possible tilting of the skyscraper that might result from changes in ground water conditions. The building is being renovated for use by Deutsche Bahn.

61 | Dresdner Bank

Adresse: Jürgen-Ponto-Platz 1
Stadtteil: Bahnhofsviertel
Erbauung: 1978–1980, Renovierung 2009/10
Architekten: H. G. Beckert, G. Becker

Ostzeile Römerberg | 62

Frankfurts Altstadt wurde zu weiten Teilen im Zweiten Weltkrieg zerstört. Nach langer Kontroverse wurde die Ostzeile des Römerbergs mit Kopien der historischen Fachwerkbauten neu bebaut. Zeichnungen und Fotografien dienten als Vorlage. Alte Hölzer und Mainsandstein wurden handwerklich bearbeitet, um eine möglichst hohe Authentizität herzustellen. Der Große Engel (Original 1457, linkes Eckgebäude) ist mit seinen von Stockwerk zu Stockwerk überragenden Etagen typisch für das alte Frankfurt. Der südlich an die Ostzeile anschließende Schwarze Stern (Original 1600) ist eines der schönsten Renaissancehäuser in Frankfurt.

EAST SIDE OF RÖMERBERG *The historic centre of Frankfurt was largely destroyed during the Second World War. After a lengthy controversy, the east side of the city hall square, which is called Römerberg, was rebuilt with copies of the historical half-timbered buildings. Drawings and photographs were used as models. Old lumber and Main sandstone were handcrafted in order to achieve as much authenticity as possible. The "Große Engel" building (the original was built in 1457, left) with each floor overhanging the one below is typical of Frankfurt of old. The "Schwarze Stern" building (right) is one of the most beautiful Renaissance edifices built around 1600 in Frankfurt.*

Adresse: Römerberg | **Stadtteil:** Altstadt | **Erbauung:** 1983-1984
Architekten: Ernst Schirmacher, Klaus Peter Henrici, Karl-Georg Geiger

Die Neukonzeption des Messegeländes geht auf den städtebaulichen Plan von Oswald Mathias Ungers zurück. Die Gestaltung im Stil der Postmoderne prägt das Gelände bis heute. Das Torhaus, mit seinem den Himmel spiegelnden Glaskern, der symbolhaft als Tor Frankfurts in die Welt steht, war lange Wahrzeichen der Messe. Die Galleria, die Idee eines Kaufhauses aufnehmend, ist der westliche Eingang. Die rot verkleidete Halle 9 bezieht sich auf die historischen Steinhäuser Frankfurts.

TRADE FAIR GATEHOUSE,
TRADE FAIR HALL 9 AND GALLERIA

The origin of the new concept for the Trade Fair Grounds was the urban planning

63 | Messetorhaus, Messehalle 9 und Galleria

concept of Oswald Mathias Ungers. The design in the Postmodernism style is still characteristic for the Trade Fair Grounds today. The "Torhaus" (Gatehouse), which symbolises the Trade Fair as Frankfurt's gateway to the world, was the landmark of the Trade Fair for a long time. The Galleria, which incorporates the concept of the department store, is the western entrance to the Trade Fair Grounds. Hall 9 with its red facing is an allusion to the historical stone buildings of Frankfurt.

Adresse: Messegelände
Stadtteil: Bockenheim
Erbauung: 1980–1984
Architekt: Oswald Mathias Ungers

Kunsthalle Schirn | 64

Als Ergebnis des letzten Architektenwettbewerbs für die Bebauung des Dom-Römerareals entstand die Kunsthalle Schirn. Der Name bezieht sich auf die historischen offenen Verkaufsstände der Frankfurter Metzger. Die Arkadengänge sowie der symbolhafte Tisch nehmen dieses Motiv auf. Die helle Sandsteinverkleidung kontrastiert mit dem Rotsandstein des Doms. Das Bauvolumen wurde lange als zu mächtig neben der filigranen Fassade des Doms kritisiert. Das 140 Meter lange Gebäude wird als Ausstellungshalle und Musikschule genutzt.

SCHIRN ART EXHIBITION HALL *The art exhibition hall - "Kunsthalle Schirn" - was created as the result of the last architectural competition for the development of the area between the Römer, i.e. city hall, and the Cathedral. The name is a reference to the historical open-air stalls of Frankfurt's butchers. The arcaded passages as well as the symbolic table incorporate that motif. The light-coloured sandstone sheathing contrasts with the red sandstone of the cathedral. For a long time the volume of the structure was criticised as being too overwhelming so close to the delicate façade of the cathedral. The 140 metres long building is used as an exhibition hall and a music school.*

Adresse: Römerberg | **Stadtteil:** Altstadt | **Erbauung:** 1983–1985
Architekten: Dietrich Bangert, Bernd Jansen, Stefan Scholz, Axel Schultes

65 | Stadthauszeile Saalgasse

In ost-westlicher Richtung sind Stadthäuser entstanden die, in Proportion und Struktur, an die gotische Altstadt erinnern sollen. Im Hochparterre befinden sich die Geschäftsräume, im ersten Stock die „Beletage", darüber die privaten Räume und auf dem Dach das „Belvederchen", der Dachbalkon mit schöner Aussicht. Die Fassadengestaltung nimmt die Fachwerkstruktur der Altstadt ebenso auf wie Figuren und Zierelemente aus der Vorkriegszeit.

SAALGASSE TOWNHOUSE ENSEMBLE *The townhouses were constructed along an east-to-west axis; their proportions and structure are intended to be reminiscent of the historical Gothic medieval centre. The raised ground floor houses the commercial premises, and the first upper floor is the "bel étage". Above that there are private rooms and on the roof a small "Belvederchen" element that is a roof balcony offering a beautiful view. The design of the façade incorporates the half-timbered style of the historic medieval centre as well as figures and decorative elements originating in the pre-war era.*

Adresse: Saalgasse 2–28 | **Stadtteil:** Altstadt | **Erbauung:** 1984
Architekten: u. a. Nr. 6 Berghof, Lande, Rang, Nr. 8 Gerkan, Marg, Nr. 10 Mäckler, Nr. 18 Moore, Nr. 22 Natali, Nr. 28 Heinrici, Geiger

Museum für Moderne Kunst | 66

Das „Tortenstück" genannte Gebäude nutzt den gesamten Raum des Straßendreiecks. Die Fassade in Putz und Sandstein bezieht sich auf die historischen Baumaterialien Frankfurts. Die Museumsräume werden traditionell über das Dach beleuchtet. Das Innere des Hauses schafft mit seinen Balkons, Treppen, Durchgängen, Emporen und der Lichtführung immer wieder neue Eindrücke in den eigentlichen Ausstellungsräumen.

MUSEUM OF MODERN ART *The building, which has been nicknamed the „slice of cake", fills the entire space of the triangular block. The façade rendered in stucco and sandstone is an allusion to the historical construction materials used in Frankfurt. The interior rooms of the museum are illuminated traditionally through the roof. The interior of the building – with its balconies, staircases, passageways and platforms and the lighting concept – constantly conjures up new impressions in the actual exhibition rooms.*

Adresse: Domstraße 10 | **Stadtteil:** Altstadt | **Erbauung:** 1987–1991
Architekt: Hans Hollein

Der 257 Meter hohe Messeturm stellt einen Maßstabssprung der Frankfurter Hochhäuser dar. Aus einem quadratischen Sockel erhebt sich das schlanke Bauwerk mit seiner charakteristischen Pyramidenspitze. Der sechs Meter tiefe Büroraum schließt sich ringförmig um den Technikschacht mit 26 Aufzügen, Treppenhäusern und dem Versorgungsbereich. Der Stahlbetonbau ist mit einer vorgehängten Fassade aus schwedischem Granit verkleidet. Die bleistiftartige Architektur zitiert amerikanische Hochbauten des Art déco.

TRADE FAIR TOWER

The 257 metres tall "Messeturm" represents a benchmark leap among

67 | Messeturm

Frankfurt's skyscrapers. From its square plinth, the slim structure thrusts upwards with its characteristic pyramid point. The 6 metres deep office space is arranged in a ring encircling the services shaft including 26 elevators and stairways as well as utilities and disposal facilities. The reinforced concrete structure was sheathed with a curtain-type façade using Swedish granite. The pencil-shaped architecture is an allusion to American high-rise buildings of the Art Deco era.

Adresse: Friedrich-Ebert-Anlage 49
Stadtteil: Bockenheim
Erbauung: 1988–1991
Architekten: Helmuth Jahn, Charles Franklin Murphy

Kindertagesstätte KT 130 | 68

Die burgenhaft romantisierende Kindertagesstätte mit ihrer vergoldeten Zwiebelturmspitze entstand auf dem ehemaligen Werksgelände der Heddernheimer Metallwerke. Die Philosophie des Architekten, der Erde entzogene Fläche mit einem erdbedeckten Bauwerk „zurückzugeben", wurde durch den verseuchten Baugrund zunächst infrage gestellt. Erst nach Reinigung des Erdreiches konnte das Gebäude benutzt werden. Hundertwassers Idee, keine geraden Linien zu bauen, wurde ebenfalls umgesetzt.

CHILDREN'S DAYCARE FACILITY *This children's daycare facility with its romantic castle-like flair and a tower topped by a gilded onion dome was built on the former factory grounds of the Heddernheimer Metallwerke. Initially, the philosophy of the architect focussing on "giving back" to the earth the areas that have been stolen from it with an earth-covered structure was put into question because of contamination in the foundation soil. It was only possible to use the building after the soil had been cleaned. Hundertwasser's concept of building without any straight lines was also realised.*

Adresse: Kupferhammer 93 | **Stadtteil:** Heddernheim | **Erbauung:** 1989
Architekt: Friedensreich Hundertwasser

69 | Museum Judengasse

Der Neubau der Frankfurter Stadtwerke wurde über den Fundamenten der ehemaligen Judengasse errichtet. Von den 17 entdeckten Kellerresten wurden fünf in das Museum integriert. Diese zeigen die großen sozialen, räumlichen und baulichen Unterschiede der Ghettobauten. Der Neubau des Stadtwerke-Kundenzentrums schließt eine schwierige städtebauliche Situation der Nachkriegszeit ab.

JUDENGASSE MUSEUM *Even before commencing the excavation work for the new building, it was clear that the remains of the historical ghetto of Frankfurt's Jews would be found at this location. Only 5 of the 17 vestiges of cellars that were found have been integrated into the museum. These reveal the great social, spatial and structural differences between the ghetto buildings. The new building constructed for the municipal utility's customer centre brings closure to a difficult urban planning situation that existed in the post-war era.*

Adresse: Kurt-Schumacher-Straße 10 | **Stadtteil:** Innenstadt | **Erbauung:** 1990
Architekt: Ernst Gisel

Die Hochhausachse der Mainzer Landstraße wird durch das auch „Westend 1“ genannte 208 Meter hohe Gebäude betont. Zeittypisch ist die Gliederung in einen Sockel, eine Säule und ein Kapitell. Seine städtebauliche Wirkung entfaltet das Haus durch den herausragenden Strahlenkranz an der Spitze, der eine Krone symbolisiert. Das Gebäude erhält durch den hellen Naturstein und die weiß beschichtete Metallverkleidung eine elegante Fernwirkung.

DZ Bank

The high-rise axis along Mainzer Landstraße is accentuated by the 208 metres tall building, which is also called "Westend 1". The integration into a plinth, a

DZ Bank | 70

column and a capital are typical of the era. The building achieves its urban planning effect by means of the halo at the top of the structure, symbolising a crown and coronations. The light-coloured natural stone and the white coated metal cladding give the building its elegant appearance from a distance.

Adresse: Mainzer Landstraße 58
Stadtteil: Westend
Erbauung: 1990–1993
Architekten: Eugen Kohn, William Pedersen, Fox, W. Nägele, D. Hofmann, J. Tiedemann

71 | Behördenzentrum

Hinter der ehemaligen preußischen Gutleutkaserne von 1877 wurde auf dem ehemaligen Exerzierplatz das Behördenzentrum für fünf Finanzämter und weitere Einrichtungen des Landes Hessen gebaut. Auf dem kammartigen, mit Naturstein verkleideten Gebäude befinden sich farbige Kegel, die den Besuchern den Weg weisen sollen. Das Gebäude stellt auch eine Wegebrücke vom Hauptbahnhof in das Gutleutviertel her.

PUBLIC ADMINISTRATION CENTRE *The public administration centre for five tax offices and additional facilities of the State of Hessen was constructed on what used to be the parade grounds behind the former Prussian barracks of the Gutleutkaserne, which was built in 1877. In order to facilitate orientation and show visitors where to go, coloured cones have been placed on the top of the comb-type structure, which is sheathed in natural stone. The building also forms a footpath connection between the Main Railway Station and the Gutleutviertel district.*

Adresse: Gutleutstraße 116–124 | **Stadtteil:** Gutleutviertel | **Erbauung:** 1990–1994
Architekten: P. Scheele, J. Zimmer

Die strengen geometrischen Formen des nur 114 Meter hohen Gebäudes und das schwarze herausragende Dach, das an japanische Steinlaternen erinnert, geben dem Turm eine besondere Wirkung. Die Gliederung der Fassade ist als doppelte Tatamimatte (japanische Bodenmatte) von 90 x 180 Zentimeter gestaltet. Dieses Modul ist ein wichtiges Element der japanischen Architektur. Die Fassade aus unterschiedlich poliertem Naturstein betont die Wirkung.

Japan Center

The building is only 114 metres tall, but the austere geometric shapes and the black protruding roof that is reminiscent of Japanese stone lanterns give the tower

Japan Center | 72

a very special effect. The façade is designed to emulate a double Tatami mat (Japanese floor mat) measuring 90 x 180 cm. That modular grid is an important element of Japanese architecture. The façade rendered in different types of polished natural stone additionally underscores the effect.

Adresse: Taunustor 2–4
Stadtteil: Innenstadt
Erbauung: 1993–1996
Architekten: Joachim Ganz, Walter Rolfes

73 | Kastor und Pollux

Als zwei auf einer Seite leicht gebogene Scheiben bilden die Häuser Kastor (94 Meter) und Pollux (130 Meter) das Forum Frankfurt und damit die Flanken eines Platzes. Mit den in Traufhöhe der Nachbarschaft eingezogenen Säulen soll sich das Ensemble in die umgebende Bebauung einfügen. Die Häuser sind mit einer vorgehängten Aluminium-Glas-Fassade und Naturstein verkleidet. Aufgeständerte Böden und abgehängte Decken erlauben eine hohe Flexibilität in der Raumaufteilung.

KASTOR AND POLLUX *The Kastor (94 metres) and Pollux (130 metres) Buildings, which are shaped like two slabs slightly curved on one side, form the Forum Frankfurt and thus the sides of a square. The columns inserted at the same height as the eaves of adjacent structures are intended to integrate the ensemble into the surrounding buildings. The structures are sheathed with a curtain-type aluminium glass façade and natural stone. Floors supported by post and beam systems and suspended ceilings permit a great deal of flexibility for partitioning the interior space.*

Adresse: Platz der Einheit 1 | **Stadtteil:** Bockenheim | **Erbauung:** 1997
Architekten: Eugen Kohn, William Pedersen, Fox, W. Nägele, D. Hofmann, J. Tiedemann

Auf einem dreieckigen Grundriss erhebt sich das 258,75 Meter hohe Gebäude. Mit der Antenne ist es fast 300 Meter hoch. Das Gebäude ist mit 111 Betonpfählen, die bis in eine Tiefe von fast 50 Metern reichen, gegründet. Spiralförmig sind neun Wintergärten um ein Atrium angeordnet. Die Fenster der Wintergärten lassen sich öffnen, sodass mit der Sauerstoffproduktion der Pflanzen und der natürlichen Luft ein kontrolliertes Klimasystem im Haus geschaffen werden kann. Die Wintergärten sind je nach Himmelsrichtung asiatisch, mediterran oder nordamerikanisch bepflanzt.

COMMERZBANK

The 258.75 metres tall building thrusts upward from a triangular footprint.

Commerzbank | 74

Including the antenna it is almost 300 metres tall. The building's foundation rests on 111 concrete piles that go down to a depth of almost 50 metres. Nine winter garden elements are arranged in a spiral around a common atrium. The windows of the winter gardens can be opened so that it is possible to create a controlled climate system within the building by means of the oxygen production of plants and natural air. The winter gardens are planted with Asian, Mediterranean or North American vegetation depending on the direction they face.

Adresse: Große Gallusstraße 17-19
Stadtteil: Innenstadt
Erbauung: 1997
Architekt: Sir Norman Foster

75 | Deutsche Nationalbibliothek

Der Neubau ersetzt die alte Deutsche Bibliothek in Frankfurt und fügt sie in den neuen deutschen nationalen Bibliotheksverbund. Auf etwa 280 Regalkilometern werden ca. 8,2 Millionen Bücher gelagert. Das Gebäude erschließt sich aus einer Mittelachse. Auf der linken Seite befinden sich die Bereiche für die öffentliche Nutzung, auf der rechten die Verwaltung und in mehreren Untergeschossen die eigentlichen Lager. Vor dem Gebäude steht eine Backsteinskulptur des dänischen Künstlers Per Kirkeby.

GERMAN NATIONAL LIBRARY *The new building replaced the old "Deutsche Bibliothek" in Frankfurt, incorporating it into the new German national library association. It has approx. 8.2 million books stored on about 280 kilometres of shelves. The building is accessed via a central axis. The areas open for use by the public are located on the left hand side and the administration is on the right, while the actual stacks are housed on several lower levels. A perforated brick sculpture by the Danish artist Per Kirkeby accentuates the front of the building.*

Adresse: Adickesallee 1 | **Stadtteil:** Nordend | **Erbauung:** 1997
Architekten: Mete Arat-Kaiser, Gisela und Dieter Kaiser

Auf dem ehemaligen Schlachthofgelände entstand in kurzer Zeit ein neues Wohnquartier für etwa 1.000 Bewohner. Entlang des Mains wurden Solitärbauten in sehr unterschiedlicher Gestaltung errichtet. Städtebaulicher Abschluss ist das von Mäckler außen gestaltete Colosseo und der von Kohlhof entworfene 88 Meter hohe Wohn- und Hotelbau. Das Hochhaus ist mit einer Klinkerfassade und 126 expressionistischen Goldknöpfen versehen und erinnert an amerikanische Hochbauten der 1920 Jahre.

MAIN PLAZA + DEUTSCHHERRNVIERTEL

A new residential district to house about 1,000 residents was created within a short period of time on the former grounds of the

Main Plaza und Deutschherrnviertel | 76

slaughterhouse. Free-standing structures with a wide variation in design were built along the Main River. As far as urban planning is concerned, the final touch is the Colosseo, the exterior of which was designed by C. Mäckler, and the 88 m residential and hotel building designed by H. Kohlhof. The high-rise has a clinker brick veneer and is adorned with 126 expressionistic gold knobs: it is reminiscent of the American high-rise buildings built in the twenties.

Adresse: Deutschherrnufer, Gerbermühlstr.
Stadtteil: Sachsenhausen
Erbauung: 1997–2001
Architekten: Thomas Bock, Hans Kollhoff, Christian Muschalek, Christoph Mäckler, Fritz Novotny, Arthur Mähner

77 | Unionsgelände

Den Auftakt des Wandels entlang der Hanauer Landstraße bildete der Umbau des Geländes der alten Union-Brauerei. Um einen kleinen Innenplatz gruppieren sich neben der alten Brauhalle, dem Schalanderhaus und dem Getreidesilo Neubauten, die bewusst einer neuen Architektursprache folgen und dennoch ein Ensemble ergeben. Der Komplex wird für Büros, Praxen, Autohandel, Diskotheken und Veranstaltungen genutzt.

UNION BREWERY PROPERTY *The kick-off of the transformation that has taken place along Hanauer Landstraße was the conversion of the property of the old Union Brewery. In addition to the old brewery hall, the Schalander building and the grain silo, new buildings that consciously incorporate a new architectural idiom have been arranged around a small interior square, forming an eclectic ensemble. The complex is used for offices, medical practices, a car dealership, discotheques and events.*

Adresse: Hanauer Landstraße 184–198 | **Stadtteil:** Ostend | **Erbauung:** 1998–2001
Architekt: Michael Landes

Hinter einem Sockel, der zum Teil von einer historischen Fassade stammt, erhebt sich das Hochhaus bis zu einer öffentlichen Aussichtsplattform in 200 Metern. Die Antenne erhöht das Gebäude um weitere 40 Meter. Das Hochhaus besteht aus zwei Teilen, die sich mit einem runden und einem quadratischen Grundriss um den Versorgungskern ziehen. Die Fenster der vorgehängten Fassade lassen sich öffnen.
Im Main Tower befindet sich Europas höchstes Fernsehstudio.

MAIN TOWER

Behind a plinth that was to some extent originally part of a historical facade, the skyscraper thrusts upward to a public

Main Tower | 78

observation deck at a height of 200 metres. The antenna adds another 40 metres to the height of the building. The skyscraper consists of two sections with a round and a square footprint that enclose the utility services core. The windows in the curtain-type façade can be opened. The TV studio at the highest elevation in Europe is located in the high-rise building.

Adresse: Neue Mainzer Straße 52–58
Stadtteil: Innenstadt
Erbauung: 1999
Architekt: Peter Schweger

79 | Hilton

Nach langem kommunalem Streit wurde das 1960 fertiggestellte und unter Denkmalschutz stehende Stadtbad Mitte umgebaut und durch einen Hotelbau ergänzt. Die beiden leicht geschwungenen Bettenhäuser bilden im Inneren ein über die gesamte Höhe reichendes beeindruckendes Atrium mit freigestelltem Glasaufzug.

HILTON *After a lengthy municipal dispute, the "Stadtbad Mitte", a swimming pool which was completed in 1960 and which is a protected historic landmark, was remodelled and supplemented by a hotel building. The two slightly curved hotel structures form an impressive interior atrium soaring up the entire height, with an exposed glass elevator.*

Adresse: Hochstraße 4 | **Stadtteil:** Innenstadt | **Erbauung:** 1999
Architekt: John Seifert

Der Gesamtkomplex der Frankfurter Welle besteht aus der ehemaligen Merton-Villa und aus zwei Büro- und Wohngebäuden entlang des Reuterwegs und der Leerbachstraße.
Das geschwungene dreizehngeschossige Gebäude in der Geländemitte gab dem Komplex seinen Namen. Die Fassade ist in Teilen mit grünem Glas verkleidet, das einen starken Kontrast zur Nachbarschaft bildet.

FRANKFURT WAVE

The overall complex of the "Frankfurter Welle" consists of the former Merton Villa (1903 - 05, Ritter and Heßler) along Reuterweg and Leerbachstraße and two office and residential buildings.

Frankfurter Welle | 80

The meandering thirteen-storey building in the middle of the property gave the building its name. Parts of the façade are sheathed in green glass, thus creating a stark contrast with the neighbourhood.

Adresse: An der Welle
Stadtteil: Westend
Erbauung: 1903-1905 (Merton-Villa); 2001 (Frankfurter Welle)
Architekten: Ritter, Heßler (Merton-Villa); JKS Architekten (Frankfurter Welle)

81 | Allianz

Exponiert an der Friedensbrücke steht der sechsgeschossige kammartige Bau mit dem 16 Etagen umfassenden, verglasten Hochhaus. Das Gebäude wird von einer „Magistrale“ im ersten Stockwerk erschlossen. Zur Gartenstraße ist das Gebäude geschlossen, zum Main bilden die fünf Querriegel kleine Innenhöfe.

ALLIANZ *The six-storey comb-like structure including a small 16-storey, glassed-in high-rise building is located in an exposed location by the Friedensbrücke bridge. The building is accessed via a "Magistrale" (main access corridor) on the first upper level. The building is enclosed on the Gartenstraße side; on the side facing the Main River, 5 transversal elements form small interior courtyards.*

Adresse: Theodor-Stern-Kai 1 | **Stadtteil:** Sachsenhausen | **Erbauung:** 2001
Architekten: HPP Hentrich, Petschnigg & Partner

Messehalle 3 und Messeforum | 82

Zu den beeindruckendsten Großbauten Frankfurts der letzten Jahre gehört die Messehalle 3 mit ihrer freitragenden stählernen Dachkonstruktion. Das geschwungene Dach mit fünf „Höckern" überwölbt eine Fläche von 20.000 Quadratmetern. Die Stahlrohre wurden im sächsischen Plauen produziert. Es ist eine der größten Hallen Europas entstanden. Daneben befindet sich das Messeforum, als Ausstellungs- und Veranstaltungsgebäude zwischen Halle 3 und Festhalle gelegen.

TRADE FAIR HALL 3 AND TRADE FAIR FORUM *Trade Fair Hall 3 with its self-supporting steel roof construction is one of the most impressive large structures that have been built in Frankfurt in the last few years. The curved roof with five "humps" arches over an area of 20,000 sq m. The steel tubes were produced in Plauen in Saxony. It is one of the largest hall structures in Europe. The "Forum", which serves as an exhibition and event building, is located right next to it between Hall 3 and the "Festhalle" (Festival Hall).*

Adresse: Messegelände | **Stadtteil:** Bockenheim | **Erbauung:** 2001
Architekten: Nicholas Grimshaw, KSP Engel und Zimmermann

Die Umgestaltung des Westhafens von 1886 zum Wohn- und Geschäftsviertel erfolgte ab dem Jahr 2003. Der Westhafen Tower bildet den städtebaulichen Auftakt des Westhafenareals. Der runde Grundriss gibt dem Gebäude seine besondere Gestalt. Die aufwändige Fassade der Firma Gartner aus Gundelfingen, mit ihren zu öffnenden Raufenfenstern hat dem Bau den Spitznamen „Geripptes" eingetragen. Das Gebäude bezieht einen Teil seiner Kühlenergie aus dem Main.

WESTHAFEN TOWER

The conversion of the "Westhafen" area (western harbour facilities) dating back to 1886 into a residential and commercial district was implemented as of the year

83 | Westhafen Tower

2003. The Westhafen Tower serves as the urban planning overture for the Westhafen area. The round footprint gives the building its special appearance. The intricate façade by the Gartner company from Gundelfingen with its diamond-shaped windows that can be opened has given rise to the structure's nickname - "Gerippte" – the name for Frankfurt's traditional apple wine glasses with a diamond pattern. The cooling energy for the building comes from the Main.

Adresse: Westhafenplatz 1
Stadtteil: Gutleutviertel
Erbauung: 2000–2004
Architekten: schneider+schumacher, Christoph Mäckler

Der Sockelbau nimmt die Höhe und teilweise die Materialien der umliegenden Bebauung auf. Im Sockel befindet sich das English Theatre. Die beiden Hochhausteile von 113 und 130 Metern werden vom Versorgungskern von 136 Metern Höhe überragt. Die Klimatechnik nutzt die Erdwärme, auch lassen sich die Fenster des komplett verglasten Gebäudes öffnen.

GALLILEO

The plinth structure incorporates the height and to some extent the materials of the surrounding buildings. The "English Theatre" is located in the plinth section. The two high-rise sections measuring 113 metres and 130 metres in height

are surmounted by the utility services core, which is 136 metres tall. The air conditioning technology makes use of geothermal energy. The windows of the completely glassed in building can also be opened.

Adresse: Gallusanlage 7
Stadtteil: Bahnhofsviertel
Erbauung: 2002
Architekten: Fritz Novotny, Arthur Mähner und Assoziierte

Das 80 Meter hohe Hochhaus mit seiner streng gegliederten Lochfassade nimmt die Struktur des benachbarten Gewerkschaftshauses von Max Taut aus dem Jahr 1931 auf. Das Gebäude wird ringförmig von einem viergeschossigen Wohn- und Geschäftsgebäude umschlossen. Die rote Sandsteinfassade ist eine Reminiszenz an das historische Frankfurter Baumaterial.

MAIN FORUM

The 80 metres tall high-rise building with its austerely structured, perforated façade takes up the theme of the structure of the neighbouring trade union building by Max Taut, which was built in 1931. A 4-storey residential and commercial

85 | MainForum

building encircles the high-rise like a ring. The red sandstone façade recalls the historical building materials used in Frankfurt.

Adresse: Wilhelm-Leuschner-Straße 79–85
Stadtteil: Gutleutviertel
Erbauung: 2003
Architekten: Gruber + Kleine-Kraneburg

Hörsaal- und Institutsgebäude Hochschule St. Georgen | 86

Inmitten des Hochschulparks mit seinem alten Baumbestand steht ein scharf definierter Kubus, der von einem silbrig schimmernden Seilnetz umspannt wird. Er vermeidet bewusst jede eigene Formensprache, um sich in das Nebeneinander der bestehenden Gebäude mit ihren verschiedenen Baustilen zu integrieren. Sobald er – wie geplant – von wildem Wein bewachsen sein wird, bildet der grüne Würfel ein Sinnbild für die gelungene Symbiose zwischen Architektur und Natur.

Auditorium St. Georgen Amidst the Institute's park with its old tree population, you'll find a sharply defined Cube, braided by a silvery gleaming rope net. Deliberately avoiding its own element of style it integrates itself harmoniously in the side by side of the already existing buildings with their different architectural styles. As soon as it will be overgrown with Virginia creeper the cube will become a symbol for the successful symbiosis of Architecture and Nature.

Adresse: Offenbacher Landstraße 224 | **Stadtteil:** Sachsenhausen | **Erbauung:** 2004
Architekten: Kissler + Effgen Architekten

Der gesamte Komplex besteht aus drei Gebäuden: der so genannten Holzmann Villa, dem 151 Meter hohen, halbrund geschwungenen Hochhaus und einem sich dahinter anschließenden Wohn- und Geschäftshaus. Durch eine transparente Halle sind die neoklassizistische Villa und das komplett verglaste Hochhaus miteinander verbunden. Ein Teil des Energiebedarfs des gesamten Areals wird durch Erdwärme gedeckt.

Skyper

The whole complex encompasses three buildings: The so-called Holzmann Villa, which was built in 1915, the 151 metres high rising skyscraper, completely enclosed in glass, and a six-storey residential

87 | Skyper

building. The neoclassical villa and the elegantly curved semicircular skyscraper are connected through a glass atrium. The building complex derives part of its energy requirements from geothermal energy.

Adresse: Taunusanlage 1
Stadtteil: Bahnhofsviertel
Erbauung: 1915 (Holzmann-Villa); 2001 (Skyper)
Architekt: Helmut W. Joos (Skyper)

Commerzbank Arena | 88

Anstelle des alten Waldstadions, dessen Geschichte bis in das Jahr 1925 zurückging, ist die heutige Arena bereits der vierte Neubau. Sie fasst 52.000 Besucher und zählt zu den zehn größten Stadien Deutschlands. Die zwei Rangebenen sind horizontal von 74 Logen getrennt. Zu den technischen Besonderheiten gehört das Stahl-Seil-Membran-Innendach oder Zeltdach von 37.500 Quadratmetern, das aus dem Videowürfel heraus aufgespannt werden kann. Es ist das größte seiner Art.

COMMERZBANK ARENA *The present arena, which replaced the old "Waldstadion" that was built in the year 1925, is already the fourth new structure. The stadium can accommodate almost 52,000 spectators and is one of the ten largest stadiums in Germany. The two tier levels are horizontally separated by 74 boxes. The special technical features include the steel cable membrane interior roof or tent roof (37,500 sq m) that can be opened up from the video cube. It is the largest roof of its kind.*

Adresse: Mörfelder Landstraße 362 | **Stadtteil:** Sachsenhausen | **Erbauung:** 2002–2005
Architekten: gmp von Gerkan, Marg und Partner

89 | Baseler Oval

Das ovale Hochhaus wurde wegen seiner die Nachbarschaft ignorierenden Form heftig kritisiert. Dennoch bildet das außergewöhnliche Gebäude ein markantes Entree in das Bahnhofsviertel. Der mit Naturstein braunbeige verkleidete Bau stiftet einen deutlichen Kontrast zur gründerzeitlichen Bebauung des Baseler Platzes.

BASELER OVAL *The oval high-rise building was strongly criticised because of its shape, which does not reflect its environment in any way. Nevertheless, the unusual building forms a striking entrée to the Bahnhofsviertel area surrounding the main railway station. The structure sheathed in brown/beige natural stone offers a perceptible contrast to the Wilhelminian buildings on Baseler Platz.*

Adresse: Baseler Straße 10 | **Stadtteil:** Gutleutviertel | **Erbauung:** 2004
Architekten: Albert Speer und Partner

Radisson Blu | 90

Die städtebauliche Erweiterung Bockenheims erfolgte nach Süden bis zur Theodor-Heuss-Allee. Große Solitärbauten begrenzen den Stadtteil. Das als runde, blau verglaste Scheibe gebaute Hotel bezieht sich architektonisch nicht auf das Umfeld. Der 87 Meter hohe Bau bildet den Endpunkt der Neubauachse.

RADISSON BLU *The urban planning expansion of Bockenheim has extended the district in a southerly direction as far as Theodor-Heus Allee. Large free-standing buildings delineate the limits of the city district. The hotel, which was constructed in the form of a round, blue, glass-enclosed slab, does not make any reference to its environment. The 87 metres tall structure forms the terminal point of the new construction axis.*

Adresse: Franklinstraße 65 | **Stadtteil:** Bockenheim | **Erbauung:** 2005
Architekt: John Seifert

91 | Portikus

Die Alte Brücke in Frankfurt ist sicher das bedeutendste weltliche Bauwerk der Stadt. Die Brücke war von alters her durch verschiedenen Nutzbauten wie Mühlen ergänzt worden. Diese historische Idee nimmt das schlanke, hohe, an ein gotisches Altstadtgebäude erinnernde Ausstellungshalle Portikus wieder auf. Das Gebäude ist mit einem ochsenblutroten, kannelierten Putz versehen. In den nächsten Jahren wird auf der gegenüberliegenden Inselseite ein ebenfalls an historischen Vorbildern orientiertes Gebäude entstehen.

PORTIKUS *The bridge in Frankfurt called Alte Brücke is undoubtedly the city's most significant secular structure. From time out of mind the bridge has been supplemented with various utility structures such as mills. This historical concept was the inspiration for the tall, slim structure of the "Portikus" exhibition hall, which is reminiscent of a historical Gothic building. The structure has been sheathed in fluted stucco finished in oxblood red. On the opposite side of the island, a building that will also be modelled after historical examples is to be constructed in the next few years.*

Adresse: Alte Brücke 2, Maininsel | **Stadtteil:** Sachsenhausen | **Erbauung:** 2005–2006
Architekt: Christoph Mäckler

Haus am Dom | 92

Der Neubau des Hauses am Dom ergänzt und erweitert das historische, im Stil des Bauhauses errichtete Zollamt nach Süden. Der neue Kopfbau ist durch einen Gebäudeeinschnitt deutlich vom Altbau getrennt. Das Bildungszentrum der Katholischen Kirche ist zugleich Erweiterung des Dommuseums. Die historische Zollhalle wird heute als Raum für Ausstellungen genutzt.

House by the Cathedral *The newly constructed building called "Haus am Dom" supplements and extends the historical customs office built in the Bauhaus style on the south side. The new front building is clearly separated from the old building by a structural indentation. The Educational Centre of the Roman Catholic Church simultaneously serves as the extension of the Cathedral Museum. Today the historical customs hall is used for exhibitions.*

Adresse: Domplatz 3 | **Stadtteil:** Altstadt | **Erbauung:** 2007
Architekten: Werner Hebebrand (Hauptzollamt); Jourdan & Müller (Haus am Dom)

93 | Westhafen – Cronstetten-Haus und Torhaus Westhafen

Zum Konzept der Westhafen City gehört eine durchmischte Sozialstruktur. Das Senioren-Wohnhaus Cronstetten-Haus nimmt die sieben- bis achtgeschossige Bebauung der Speicherstraße auf und definiert mit dem auf der Westseite anschließenden Zentralen Platz eine eindeutige Platzwand.

Das Bürohaus Torhaus Westhafen symbolisiert den Eingang in den Hafenbereich. Über das 30 Meter hohe Atrium erschließt sich das siebengeschossige Gebäude. Die Fassade besteht aus fein kanneliertem Naturstein.

WESTHAFEN – CRONSTETTEN-HAUS UND TORHAUS WESTHAFEN *Part of the concept for the "Westhafen City" is a mixed social structure. The Seniors' Residence Cronstetten-Haus incorporates the 7- to 8-storey buildings of Speicherstraße and defines a clearly demarcated side of the square on the west side of the adjacent central square called "Zentraler Platz". The "Torhaus Westhafen" office building (Westhafen Gatehouse) symbolises an entrance to the harbour area. The 7-storey building is accessed via the 30 metres tall atrium. The façade of the building is sheathed in finely fluted natural stone.*

Adresse: Speicherstraße 39-47 (Cronstetten-Haus); Speicherstrasse 57-59 (Torhaus Westhafen)
Stadtteil: Gutleutviertel | **Erbauung:** 2004-2008 | **Architekten:** Frick.Reichert Architekten (Cronstetten-Haus), Christoph Mäckler (Torhaus Westhafen)

Campus Westend der Goethe-Universität | 94

Hinter dem historischen IG Farben-Haus entstanden in der ersten Ausbaustufe um großzügige Grünflächen nach den städtebaulichen Plänen von Ferdinand Heide folgende Gebäude: Neue Mensa und Hörsaalzentrum, House of Finance, Institutsgebäude der Rechts- und Wirtschaftswissenschaften. Alle nehmen mit ihren Natursteinfassaden die Gestaltung des Altbaus auf. Im Osten des Geländes befindet sich der Rest eines mittelalterlichen Wachturmes, der in die zweite Ausbaustufe integriert werden wird.

WESTEND CAMPUS *Behind the historical IG Farben building amid spacious areas of greenery, the following buildings were constructed according to the urban planning plans of Ferdinand Heide: "Neue Mensa" (new cafeteria) and "Hörsaalzentrum" (auditorium centre) (Ferdinand Heide), House of Finance (Jan Kleihues), faculty building (Ivan Reimann). All of the buildings incorporate the design of the historical old building in their natural stone façades. In the eastern part of the grounds there are the remains of a medieval watch tower, which has been integrated into the overall complex.*

Adresse: Grüneburgplatz 1 | **Stadtteil:** Westend | **Erbauung:** 2008
Architekten: Ferdinand Heide (Neue Mensa und Hörsaalzentrum); Jan Kleihues (House of Finance); Ivan Reimann (Institutsgebäude der Rechts- und Wirtschaftswissenschaften)

95 | Messehalle 11

Ein Geländezukauf ermöglichte der Messe Frankfurt eine wesentliche Erweiterung. Das Eingangsgebäude am Ende des Neuen Dammgrabens ist als fernwirksames Tor entworfen. Die Leichtigkeit des Baus wird vom „fliegenden" in Holzbindern ausgeführten Dach der Halle 11 weitergeführt. Sie bietet 23.860 Quadratmetern Ausstellungsfläche und gewinnt ihre architektonische Offenheit durch große Glasfassaden und Balkons.

TRADE FAIR HALL 11 *The purchase of additional property made it possible for the Frankfurt Trade Fair to expand substantially. The entrance building at the end of Neuer Dammgraben has been designed to look like a gate from a distance. The airiness of the structure is continued in the roof of Hall 11, which is constructed of "flying" wooden trusses. The Hall, which encompasses 23,860 sq m of exhibition area, achieves its architectural openness by means of large glass façades and balconies.*

Adresse: Messegelände | **Stadtteil:** Bockenheim | **Erbauung:** 2009
Architekten: Rainer Hascher, Sebastian Jehle

Airrail Center | 96

Das Airrail Center ist ein 660 Meter langes und bis zu 65 Meter breites Gebäude, das zwischen den Autobahnen und über dem ICE-Bahnhof entsteht. Genutzt wird das Gebäude für Büros, Hotels, Kliniken und den Einzelhandel. Unter dem geschwungenen, an einen Paraglider erinnernden Dach des Aviation Center befinden sich zehn kammartige Gebäude, die in den Zwischenräumen zur natürlichen Belüftung und für die Lichtversorgung Gärten haben.

AIRRAIL CENTER *The Airrail Center is a 660 metres long building measuring up to 65 metres in width that is being constructed between the autobahn and another highway and above the ICE Railway Station. The utilisation of the building will include offices, hotel, hospitals and retail space.*
Aviation Center: Ten comb-like buildings are nestled under a curved roof that is reminiscent of a paraglider, with gardens in the intervening spaces to supply natural ventilation and light.

Adresse: Hugo-Eckener-Ring (Airrail Center); Airportring (Aviation Center)
Stadtteil: Flughafen | **Erbauung:** 2009 | **Architekten:** Bothe, Richter, Therani; J.S.K. (Airrail Center); Christoph Ingenhoven (Aviation Center)

97 | PalaisQuartier

Auf dem ehemaligen Gelände der Deutschen Telekom entstanden zwei Türme (ein Bürogebäude von 136 Metern und ein Hotel von 96 Metern Höhe) mit auffällig gefalteter Fassade. Durch das davor liegende und im Maßstab 1:0,96 rekonstruierte Palais Thurn und Taxis entsteht ein spannungsvoller Platz zwischen Rekonstruktion und Neubau. Die 47.000 Quadratmeter Verkaufsfläche des ebenfalls dazugehörenden Einkaufszentrums MyZeil werden von einer sich organisch aus der Fassade entwickelnden und in das Dach übergehenden Konstruktion aus unterschiedlichen Glaselementen umfasst.

PALAISQUARTIER *On the property that used to belong to Deutsche Telekom, two high-rise buildings (a 136 metres office building and a 96 metres hotel) with strikingly designed façades were created according to plans by KSP. An exciting square is being created between the reconstruction section and the new building, whereby the "Palais Thurn und Taxis" is being rebuilt on a scale of 1:0.96. Massimiliano Fuksas designed the shopping centre that has been christened "My Zeil". The 47,000 sq m of retail space are enclosed by a construction made of various glass elements that seem to grow organically out of the façade and merge into the roof.*

Adresse: Zeil 106 (MyZeil) | **Stadtteil:** Innenstadt | **Erbauung:** 2003–2009
Architekten: KSP Engel und Zimmermann (Türme und Palais); Massimiliano Fuksas (MyZeil)

Die Blockrandbebauung nimmt die Traufhöhe der gründerzeitlichen Häuser in der Nachbarschaft auf. Erst dahinter erhebt sich das 170 Meter hohe Gebäude. Der Architekt plädiert auf diese Weise abermals dafür, in historischen Kontexten Materialien zu verwenden, die mit dem Umfeld harmonieren. Die streng gerasterte Fassade aus hellem Naturstein verleiht dem Bau eine klassizistische Eleganz.

OperaTower

The perimeter block development incorporates the historical buildings in the vicinity that were built in the Wilhelminian era. The 170 metre building only rises up behind that. With this

OpernTurm | 98

building, once again Christoph Mäckler presents an argument for using materials that harmonise with the surroundings in historical contexts. The austere grid structure of the façade rendered in light-coloured natural stone imbues the structure with classicistic elegance.

Adresse: Bockenheimer Landstraße 2-4
Stadtteil: Westend
Erbauung: 2009
Architekt: Christoph Mäckler

Der Hochhausrahmenplan sieht für das Gebiet rund um den Messeturm eine weitere Verdichtung mit Hochhäusern vor. Auf dem Areal der ehemaligen Bahndirektion entsteht durch den Bauherrn Vivico Real Estate ein rund 185 Meter hohes, keilförmiges Hochhaus mit einer Aluminium-Glas-Fassade, das von einem hufeisenförmigen, mit Naturstein verkleideten Sockelgebäude umgeben ist. Die Mietfläche des Gebäudes wird rund 100.000 Quadratmeter betragen.

Tower 185

The high-rise master plan for the area foresees increased densification with high-rise buildings around the "Messeturm" (Trade Fair Tower). A 185 metre

99 | Tower 185

tall skyscraper is being built on the property formerly owned by the railway: it will consist of a horseshoe shaped plinth building sheathed in natural stone and a wedge-shaped high-rise with an aluminium-glass façade.
The rental area of the building will encompass 100,000 sq m.

Adresse: Friedrich-Ebert-Anlage 35-37
Stadtteil: Gallusviertel
Erbauung: 2008–2011
Architekt: Christoph Mäckler

Hinter der historischen Großmarkthalle soll ein etwa 180 Meter hohes, aus zwei Scheiben bestehendes Gebäude entstehen. Dazwischen wird sich ein offenes Atrium mit Wintergärten befinden. Hierdurch soll der Licht- und Lufteintrag auf allen Seiten des Hochhauses hergestellt werden. Ein umstrittener Querriegel wird die Großmarkthalle durchbrechen, die für Konferenzen und andere Nutzungen dienen soll.

European Cetral Bank – New building

A building consisting of two slabs that will be about 180 metres in height is to be built behind the historical wholesale market hall. An open atrium with winter

Europäische Zentralbank – Neubau | 100

gardens will be located between those two slabs. Their purpose is to introduce light and air into the skyscraper from all sides. A controversial transversal section will slice through the wholesale market hall, which is intended to be used for conferences and other uses.

Adresse: Sonnemannstraße
Stadtteil: Ostend
Erbauung: 2010–2014
Architekten: Wolf Prix (Coop Himmelb(l)au)

TOUREN

WALKING TOURS

TOUR 1 - Altstadt / Innenstadt klassische Sightseeingtour

Es bietet sich an, die Tour zu den wichtigsten Sehenswürdigkeiten der Altstadt auf dem **Römerberg,** Frankfurts „Gut' Stubb'", zu beginnen. Seit dem Mittelalter ist dieser Platz das Herz der Stadt, alle wichtigen Veranstaltungen fanden hier statt – vom Wochenmarkt und der berühmten Messe über Ritterturniere und Schauspielaufführungen bis zu den Festivitäten anlässlich von Wahl und Krönung der deutschen Könige und Kaiser.

Den Namen verdankt er dem auf seiner Westseite gelegenen **Rathaus Römer (Nr. 15),** dessen Fassadendekoration auf die ruhmreiche Rolle der Stadt während des Heiligen Römischen Reiches Deutscher Nation anspielt. Ein Besuch des Kaisersaals, in dem alle 52 deutschen Herrscher, von Karl dem Großen bis Franz II., in einem Gemäldezyklus verewigt sind, wird unbedingt empfohlen.

Da der „Römer" von Anfang an auch Gerichtssitz gewesen ist, steht auf seinem Vorplatz der **Justitiabrunnen.** Die heutige Göttin der Gerechtigkeit wurde 1887 geschaffen und ist eine Bronzekopie der ursprünglichen Sandsteinfigur von 1610.

Die **Alte Nikolaikirche (Nr. 3)** am südlichen Rand des Römerbergs stammt aus staufischer Zeit und wurde lange als Ratskapelle genutzt. Im Inneren sind die eindrucksvollen Grabplatten des früheren Schultheißen Siegfried zum Paradies und seiner Gattin Katharina zum Wedel aus dem beginnenden 15. Jh. zu bewundern.

Frankfurts Altstadt war bis zu ihrer Zerstörung im Zweiten Weltkrieg für ihre Fachwerkhäuser bekannt. Durch die Rekonstruktion der **Ostzeile** und des **Schwarzen Sterns (Nr. 62)** Mitte der 1980er Jahre bekommt man eine ungefähre Vorstellung vom früheren Aussehen des Römerbergs.

Wenn Sie am nördlichen Ende der Ostzeile in den Markt einbiegen, finden Sie zu Ihrer Linken gleich das **Steinerne Haus (Nr. 17).** Das Wappen über der ehemaligen Durchfahrt weist darauf hin, dass dies einst das Domizil einer Patrizierfamilie war.

Gehen Sie weiter Richtung Dom und verweilen Sie kurz an der kleinen Aussichtsplattform, von der aus man den **Archäologischen Garten** betrachten kann. An einem Modell werden Ihnen die Ruinen aus römischer und karolingischer Zeit verdeutlicht; es handelt sich um zwei Thermenanlagen einer militärischen Nachschubbasis aus dem 1./2. Jh. und um eine Königspfalz aus der Zeit um 820.

Von hier aus sehen Sie bereits den **Dom (Nr. 7).** Es lohnt sich in jedem Fall, ihn auch von innen zu besichtigen. Im Chor sind beispielsweise noch das Gestühl aus der Mitte des 15. Jhs. und der Fries mit Szenen aus dem Leben des Hl. Bartholomäus von 1427 erhalten. Auch die Wahlkapelle, in der die offizielle Wahl des deutschen Königs durch die Kurfürsten durchgeführt wurde, kann betreten werden.

An der Südseite des Doms steht das **Leinwandhaus (Nr. 13).**

Wenn Sie von hier aus die Straße Zum Pfarrturm überqueren, befinden Sie sich in der Saalgasse und betrachten rechterhand die **Stadthauszeile Saalgasse (Nr. 65).**

Kurz danach folgt auf der linken Seite der **Saalhof (Nr. 2).**

Wenn Sie den Saalhof in Richtung Main umrundet haben, schließen rechts unmittelbar der **Burnitz-** und der **Bernusbau** sowie der **Rententurm** an **(Nr. 32, 21 und 16).**

Werfen Sie noch einen Blick auf den **Eisernen Steg (Nr. 33),** der an der Stelle des alten Frankfurter Hafens errichtet wurde, bevor Sie sich am Fahrtor wieder Richtung Römerberg wenden.

T1 | 3

Links steht das einzige originale Fachwerkhaus des Altstadtkerns, das **Haus Wertheim (Nr. 19).** Nach wenigen Schritten sind Sie wieder auf dem Römerberg.

Falls Sie noch aufnahmefähig sein sollten, sind es von hier aus nur ein paar Meter zur „Wiege der deutschen Demokratie", der **Paulskirche (Nr. 29).** Überqueren Sie die nördlich des Römerbergs verlaufende Braubachstraße und halten Sie sich anschließend gleich links. Neben und gegenüber der Paulskirche befindet sich übrigens das **Alte Rathaus (Nr. 42),** also die Erweiterung der Römergebäude.

Und wenn Sie auch das letzte touristische „Must", das **Goethehaus (Nr. 26),** noch „abhaken" möchten, halten Sie sich auf der Rückseite der Paulskirche, der Berliner Straße, links, wechseln Sie die Straßenseite, überqueren Sie den Kornmarkt und gehen Sie nach wenigen Metern rechts durch die recht unscheinbare Graf de Thoranc-Passage – dann stehen Sie davor. Natürlich wird Ihnen die Besichtigung des Gebäudes, das noch über einige originale Ausstattungsstücke verfügt, dringend ans Herz gelegt.

The ideal place to start the tour of the most important sights of the medieval centre is the Römerberg, Frankfurt's "Gut' Stubb'" (i.e. front parlour). Since the Middle Ages this square has been the heart of the city. All of the important events have taken place here – from the weekly farmers' market and the famous trade fair to knights' tournaments and theatre performances, as well as the festivities on the occasion of the election and coronation of the German kings and emperors.

The square's name comes from the city hall, called **"Rathaus Römer" (No. 15)** *("Römer" is German for Romans), which is located on the west side. The decorative elements on the façade are an allusion to the illustrious role the city played during the Holy Roman Empire of the German Nation. A visit to the "Kaisersaal" (Emperor Hall); where all 52 German rulers from Charlemagne to Francis II are immortalised in a series of portraits; is definitely to be recommended.*

As the "Römer" was also the seat of a court right from the beginning, there is a fountain dedicated to Justicia - the **Justitiabrunnen** *– in front of it. The present goddess of justice was created in 1887 and is a bronze copy of the original sandstone figure made in 1610.*

The **"Alte Nikolaikirche" (No. 3)** *(Old Church of St. Nicholas) on the southern edge of the Römerberg square is from the Staufer period and for a long time it was used as the chapel of the city councillors. Inside you can admire the impressive tomb slabs of the former mayor Siegfried zum Paradies and his wife Katharina zum Wedel, which date back to the early 15th century.*

Frankfurt's medieval centre was famous for its half-timbered buildings until it was destroyed during World War II. As a result of the reconstruction of the eastern side – **"Ostzeile"** *– and the* **Schwarzer Stern (No. 62)** *building in the mid eighties, it is possible to get an approximate idea of what the Römerberg used to look like.*

If you turn onto Markt at the northern end of the eastern side of the square, you will see the **"Steinernes Haus" (No. 17)** *(Stone House) on your left right away. The coat of arms above the former gateway is an indication that this used to be the domicile of a patrician family.*

Continue on towards the Cathedral and spend a few minutes on the small viewing platform from where you can examine the **Archaeological Garden.** *There is a model that explains the ruins dating back to the Roman and Carolingian periods; these are the remains of two thermal baths from a military supply base dating to the 1st/2nd century C.E. and a royal palace from the period around 820.*

From here you can already see the **"Dom" (No. 7)** *(Cathedral). The interior is definitely worth a visit. For example, the choir still has its choir stalls dating back to the mid 15th century and a frieze with scenes from the life of St. Bartholomeus from 1427.*
You can visit the election chapel where the electors conducted the official elections of the German kings.

The **"Leinwandhaus" (No. 13)** *(House of Linen) is located on the south side of the Cathedral.*

If you proceed from here and cross the street called Zum Pfarrturm, you will reach Saalgasse and will see **"Stadthauszeile Saalgasse" (No. 65)** *(Townhouse Ensemble Saalgasse).*

Shortly after that you will come to the **Saalhof (No. 2)** *on the left hand side.*

T1 | 5

Once you have walked around the Saalhof towards the Main, immediately on the right you will see the **Burnitzbau** *and the* **Bernusbau** *as well as the* **Rententurm (No. 32, 21 und 16).**

You can take another look at the **"Eiserner Steg" (No. 33)** *bridge, which was erected at the location of the old Frankfurt harbour, before turning back towards Römerberg at Fahrtor.*

On the left is the only original half-timbered building in the medieval centre that has survived, **"Haus Wertheim" (No. 19).** *Just a few steps will take you back to the Römerberg square.*

If you should still be receptive enough, from here it is only a few metres to the "cradle of German democracy", the **Paulskirche (No. 29).** *Cross over Braubachstraße, which runs past the north side of Römerberg, and after that keep to your left. Incidentally, the* **"Altes Rathaus" (No. 42)** *(Old City Hall) is situated beside and opposite the Paulskirche, i.e. the addition built to enlarge the Römer buildings.*

And if you would also like to check off the last "tourist's must see" - the **"Goethehaus" (No. 26)** *- keep to the left behind the Paulskirche, on Berliner Straße, and cross the street. Then you cross Kornmarkt and after just a few metres you turn right and walk through the inconspicuous Graf de Thoranc Passage – then you will be find yourself right in front of it. Of course, we urgently advise you to visit the building, which still has several original items of furnishings and fittings.*

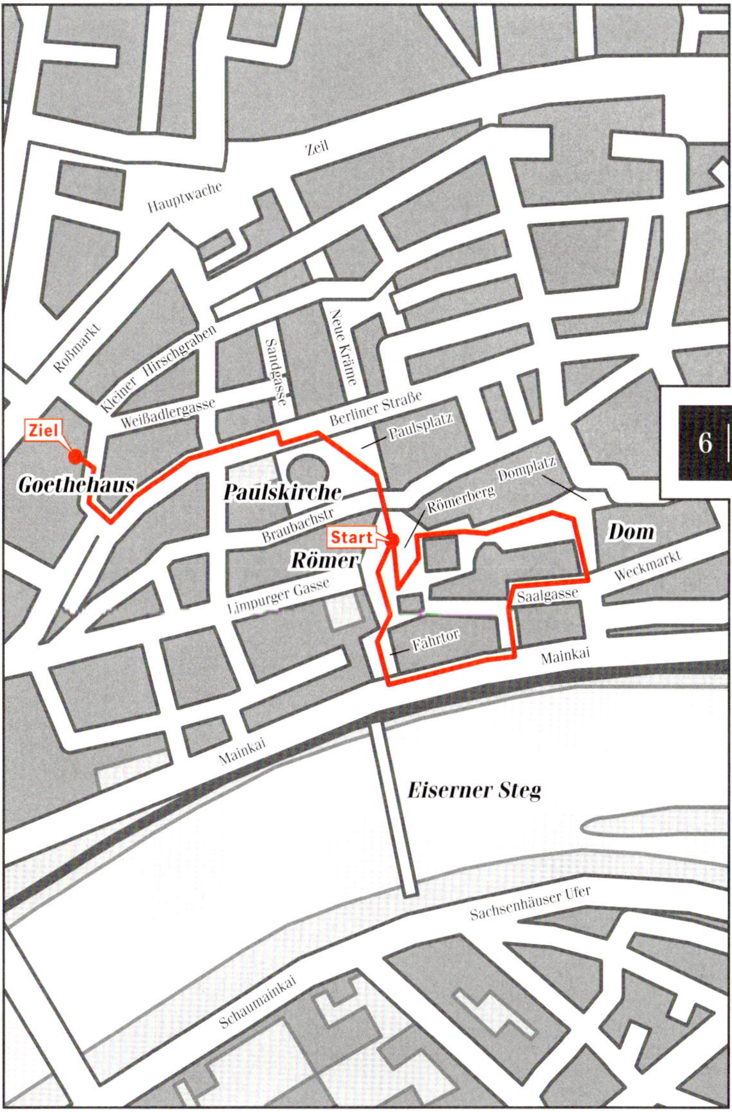

TOUR 2 - Sachsenhäuser Museumsufer

Für das Frankfurter Museumsufer, heute einer der bedeutendsten Museumsstandorte Deutschlands, wurden auf Initiative des damaligen Kulturdezernenten Hilmar Hoffmann vor allem in den 1980er Jahren vorhandene Sammlungen ausgebaut und neue Ausstellungshäuser dazugewonnen. Dafür erwarb die Stadt mehrere frühere Patriziervillen beiderseits des Mains und ließ sie entsprechend herrichten. Auf engstem Raum können nun die unterschiedlichsten Museen besichtigt werden. Eine besondere Attraktion ist das alljährlich am letzten Wochenende im August stattfindende Museumsuferfest.

Da das Sachsenhäuser Ufer die höhere „Kulturdichte" aufweist – allein hier befinden sich zehn Museen –, konzentriert sich der Spaziergang auf diese Seite des Flusses. Wie beim Rundgang durch Alt-Sachsenhausen starten wir am Deutschordenshaus, in dessen einstigem Refektorium das **Ikonenmuseum der Stadt Frankfurt am Main – Stiftung Dr. Schmidt-Voigt (Nr. 10)** untergebracht ist. Seine neuen Innenräume wurden von Oswald Mathias Ungers entworfen. Über 1.000 Ikonen auf Holz und Metall machen es zu einem der führenden Museen orthodoxer Kunst in Europa.

Wenn Sie die Walter-Kolb-Straße überquert haben, laufen Sie weiter am Main entlang, passieren den Eisernen Steg und sehen schon bald das **Museum für Angewandte Kunst** (Schaumainkai 15–17). In der klassizistischen Villa Metzler von 1804 und dem ihre Proportionen aufnehmenden Neubau aus dem Jahr 1985 von Richard Meier werden europäisches, islamisches und fernöstliches Kunsthandwerk sowie Buch- und Schriftkunst gezeigt.

Durch den Garten des Museums erreichen Sie die rückwärtige Metzlerstraße, in der das 2003 in einer ehemaligen deutsch-reformierten Kirche eröffnete **Bibelhaus – Erlebnismuseum** liegt (Metzlerstraße 19). Hier wird die Welt der Bibel und ihrer Überlieferung von den Anfängen im Nomadenzelt bis zur aktuellen Multimediawelt vorgestellt.

Zurück im Park, gelangen Sie schnell an seinem anderen Ende zum **Museum der Weltkulturen** (Schaumainkai 29–37). Es besteht aus der neobarocken Villa Andreae von 1904 und den beiden mainabwärts folgenden Gebäuden. Da das Museum über mehr als 65.000 Objekte aus Australien, Ozeanien, Afrika und Amerika verfügt, sie jedoch aus Platzmangel nur in Wechselausstellungen vorführen kann, soll es nun einen Erweiterungsbau erhalten, um seine Schätze auch dauerhaft präsentieren zu können.

Wenn Sie in westlicher Richtung weitergehen und die Schweizer Straße überqueren, kommen Sie zum **Deutschen Filmmuseum** (Schaumainkai 41). Grundstock für das weltweit erste Filmmuseum – es wurde 1984 eingeweiht – war der Nachlass des Frankfurter Kinoliebhabers Paul Sauerlaender. Neben der Geschichte des Mediums widmet man sich in dem umgebauten Gründerzeitbau auch immer wieder wichtigen Persönlichkeiten der Branche. Hier sitzt außerdem das Kommunale Kino, dessen Programm die Arbeit des Museums flankiert.

Im Nebengebäude befindet sich das **Deutsche Architekturmuseum,** das seine Exponate in dem entkernten neoklassizistischen Bau passenderweise in einem „Haus im Haus“ von Oswald Mathias Ungers vorstellt (Schaumainkai 43). Im ersten Architekturmuseum des europäischen Kontinents erfährt der Besucher Wissenswertes von der Urhütte bis zum Wolkenkratzer und kann sich in Sonderausstellungen über speziellere bauhistorische Themen informieren.

Wiederum nur wenige Schritte weiter stoßen Sie auf das **Museum für Kommunikation** (Schaumainkai 53). Die Villa de Neufville von 1891 und der Neubau des Stuttgarter Architekturbüros Günter Behnisch & Partner von 1990 sind unterirdisch miteinander verbunden. Das Museum setzt auf Interaktion, um den Besucher auf eine Reise durch die Geschichte des Postwesens und der Kommunikation mitzunehmen.

T2 | 3

An der Ecke zur Dürerstraße steht das eindrucksvolle **Städelsche Kunstinstitut (Nr. 37),** Frankfurts ältestes und berühmtestes Museum, in dem auch die 1907 gegründete Städtische Galerie untergebracht ist. Hier können Sie europäische Kunst vom 13. Jh. bis heute bestaunen. Von besonders hoher Qualität ist die Graphische Abteilung.

Eine wundervolle Ergänzung zum „Städel“, wie es im Volksmund genannt wird, ist das **Liebieghaus – Museum alter Plastik** (Schaumainkai 71). Baron Heinrich von Liebieg, ein reicher Textilfabrikant, vermachte seine an eine Burg erinnernde neoromantische Villa von Leonhard Romeis aus dem Jahr 1896 der Stadt Frankfurt – unter der Bedingung, hier ein Kunstmuseum einzurichten. 1908 erhielt es einen Galerietrakt, der 1990 durch das Architektenteam Scheffler/Warschauer erweitert wurde. Es beherbergt eine der bedeutendsten Skulpturensammlungen Europas, deren Werke einen umfassenden Überblick von der Antike bis zum Klassizismus garantieren.

Das **Museum Giersch** bildet den Abschluss der wie Perlen an einer Schnur aufgereihten Sachsenhäuser Ausstellungshäuser (Schaumainkai 83). Das Frankfurter Stifterehepaar Karin und Carlo Giersch finanzierte die Sanierung der alten Villa Holzmann von 1910. Seit dem Jahr 2000 widmet man sich hier der Erforschung und Präsentation von Kunst im

Rhein-Main-Gebiet, womit eine Lücke im kulturellen Angebot der Region geschlossen wurde.

Wenn Sie jetzt noch Kondition haben sollten, können Sie gern zum Holbeinsteg zurückkehren und sich die Frankfurter Seite des Museumsufers vornehmen, wobei nur das **Jüdische Museum** (Untermainkai 14–15) und das **Historische Museum** (Saalgasse 19) unmittelbar am Main situiert sind, während das **Archäologische Museum** (Karmelitergasse 1), das **Dommuseum** (Domplatz 1), das **Museum für Moderne Kunst** (Domstraße 10) und das **Museum Judengasse** (Kurt-Schumacher-Str. 10) jeweils etwas zurückgesetzt liegen.

WALKING TOUR - SACHSENHAUSEN MUSEUM EMBANKMENT

For Frankfurt's "Museumsufer", the array of museums on the embankment that is one of the most significant museum locations in Germany, above all in the eighties existing collections were enlarged on the initiative of Hilmar Hoffmann – who was at that time the head of the cultural office – and new exhibition buildings were acquired. To this end, the city purchased several former patrician villas on both sides of the Main and had them remodelled accordingly. Now it is possible to tour the most various of museums within a very small area. One special attraction is the "Museumsuferfest" (Museum Embankment Festival), which is held every year on the last weekend in August.

As the Sachsenhausen embankment has a higher "cultural density" – ten museums are situated at that location alone – the walking tour concentrates on that side of the river. Just like with the walking tour through Alt-Sachsenhausen, we start at the "Deutschordenshaus": in its former refectory is housed the **Icon Museum of the City of Stadt Frankfurt am Main – Stiftung Dr. Schmidt-Voigt (No. 10).** *The new interiors were designed by Oswald Mathias Ungers. Over 1,000 icons on wood and metal make it one of Europe's leading museums for Orthodox art.*

When you have crossed Walter-Kolb-Straße, continue along the Main. You go past the "Eiserner Steg" bridge and then you will soon see the **"Museum für Angewandte Kunst"** *(Museum of Applied Arts) (Schaumainkai 15-17). European, Islamic and Oriental arts and crafts as well as book art and calligraphy are exhibited in the classicistic Villa Metzler from 1804 and the new building by Richard Meier built in the year 1985, which incorporates the same proportions.*

After passing through the garden of the museum you will reach the street behind – Metzlerstraße – where the **Bibelhaus – Erlebnismuseum** *(Bible House – Experience Museum), which opened up in a former German Reformed church (Metzlerstraße 19),* is located. It presents the world of the bible and its writings - from the early beginnings in the nomadic period until today's multimedia world. Returning to the park, at the other end you will quickly reach the **"Museum der Weltkulturen"** (Museum of World Cultures) (Schaumainkai 29-37). It consists of the neo-baroque Villa Andreae from 1904 as well as the next two buildings downriver from it. As the museum has more than 65,000 exhibits from Australia, Oceania, Africa and America, but it has only been able to present them in rotating exhibitions because of the lack of space, there are now plans for an addition to enable the museum to present its treasures on a permanent basis.

If you continue to head to the west and cross Schweizer Straße, you will reach the **"Deutsches Filmmuseum"** (German Film Museum) (Schaumainkai 41). The first film museum worldwide was officially opened in 1984: the basis for it was the estate of Paul Sauerlaender, a movie aficionado from Frankfurt. Besides the history of the medium, the museum in the remodelled Wilhelminian building also regularly devotes attention to important figures in the film industry. It is also the location of the municipal movie theatre, the programme of which supports the work of the museum.

The building next door houses the **"Deutsches Architekturmuseum"** (German Architecture Museum), which fittingly presents its exhibits in the gutted neo-classicistic building in a "house within a house" designed by Oswald Mathias Ungers (Schaumainkai 43). In the first museum of architecture on the European continent, visitors find out a great deal that is worth knowing about everything from prehistoric huts to skyscrapers and can learn about special historic building themes in special exhibitions.

Just a few steps further on we will reach the **"Museum für Kommunikation"** (Museum for Communications) (Schaumainkai 53). The Villa de Neufville, which was built in 1891, and the new building of the Stuttgart architects' office Günter Behnisch & Partner built in 1990 are connected with each other underground. The museum banks on interaction in order to take visitors on a journey through the history of postal services and communications.

The corner of Dürerstraße is the location of the impressive **"Städelsches Kunstinstitut" (No. 37)** (Städel Museum of Art), Frankfurt's oldest and most famous museum. It also houses the Städtische Galerie (City Gallery), which was founded in 1907 (Schaumainkai 63, see No. 37 of the individual edifices). You can admire European art dating from the 13th century to the present. The Department of Graphic Art is of especially high quality.

The Liebieghaus – Museum alter Plastik *(Museum of Historic Sculpture) (Schaumainkai 71) is a wonderful supplement to the "Städel", as it is usually called by the people of Frankfurt. Baron Heinrich von Liebieg, a wealthy textile manufacturer, left his castle-like Neo-Romantic villa designed by Leonhard Romeis, which was built in the year 1896, to the City of Frankfurt on the condition that an art museum be set up there. In 1908 a gallery wing was added, which the Scheffler/Warschauer team of architects enlarged in 1990. It houses one of Europe's most important collections of sculptures, the works of which offer a comprehensive overview from antiquity until the age of Classicism.*

The **"Museum Giersch"** *is the final element in the row of exhibition venues in Sachsenhausen, like pearls in a necklace (Schaumainkai 83). Karin and Carlo Giersch, the Frankfurt couple who were the founders, financed the renovation of the old Villa Holzmann, which was built in 1910. Since the year 2000 the museum has devoted itself to the research and presentation of art in the Rhine-Main area, which has filled a gap in the cultural options offered in the region.*

If you still feel energetic enough, you can return to Holbeinsteg and tackle the Frankfurt side of the Museum Embankment. However, the only museums located directly on the Main are the **Jüdisches Museum** *(Jewish Museum) (Untermainkai 14-15) and the* **"Historisches Museum"** *(Historical Museum) (Saalgasse 19), while the* **"Archäologisches Museum"** *(Archaeological Museum) (Karmelitergasse 1), the* **Dommuseum** *(Cathedral Museum) (Domplatz 1), the* **"Museum für Moderne Kunst"** *(Museum of Modern Art) (Domstraße 10) and the* **"Museum Judengasse"** *(Kurt-Schumacher-Straße 10) are situated further away from the river.*

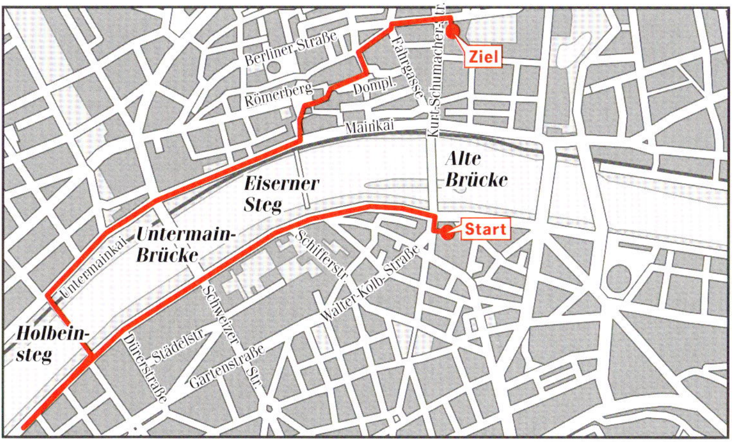

TOUR 3 - Klassizismus

Dieser Rundgang stellt Ihnen eine bedeutende Zeit der Frankfurter Architektur vor. Frankfurt war im Wesentlichen bis 1800 von gotischen Gebäuden geprägt. Einen ersten Aufbruch in den Klassizismus gab es mit der Stadterweiterung nach 1780, in das sogenannte Fischerfeld und mit dem Neubau der Paulskirche.

Unser Rundgang beginnt an der **Paulskirche (Nr 29).** Goethe meinte sinngemäß über das Gebäude: ein richtiger Bau am falschen Platz. Ihn störte der starke Kontrast zwischen damals „Modernem" und der die Kirche umgebenden gotischen Stadt.

Gehen Sie über den Römerberg bis zum **Mainkai 40,** neben der Leonhardskirche, befindet sich dieses kleine Wohnhaus von 1840. Es gehört wie alle Gebäude des Mainufers aus der Zeit nach 1800 zu den weiß gestrichenen, das Mainufer damals prägenden Bauwerken. Nach Westen, dem Mainlauf folgend, gelangen Sie zur **Villa Schlosser** (Untermainkai 4). Das ursprünglich von J.F. C. Hess 1823 errichtete Haus ist ein weiteres Beispiel der Villen des Frankfurter Großbürgertums entlang des Flusses.

Ebenfalls von Hess entworfene Gebäude sehen Sie mit den **Hausnummern 12 - 14.** Den Abschluss dieser Reihe stellt das Rothschild Palais dar. Der 1821 geschaffene Bau sowie die Erweiterung durch F. Rumpf von 1849 beherbergen heute das Jüdische Museum Frankfurt.

Folgen Sie dem Untermainkai und wechseln Sie über den Holbeinsteg die Mainseite. Folgen Sie links dem Schaumainkai bis zur **Villa Metzler** (Schaumainkai 15), ein Gartenhaus von 1802, das für die Bankiersfamilie um 1860 um ein Stockwerk nach klassizistischen Proportionen erhöht wurde.

Folgen Sie dem Main und queren Sie über die Alte Brücke auf die Frankfurter Seite. Nach rechts beginnt die „Schöne Aussicht" Hier lassen sich in den Hinterhöfen der parallel verlaufenden Straße **„Hinter der Schönen Aussicht"** etliche Rest der Bebauung um 1800 entdecken, weitgehend erhalten ist das Haus **Schützenstraße 1** von 1820.

Gehen Sie bis zur Ignatz-Bubis-Brücke. Gegenüber liegt das prominenteste Beispiel des Klassizismus nach den Plänen von J.F.C. Hess: die durch Christopf Mäckler, wiederaufgebaute **Stadtbibliothek (Nr 30).**

Dahinter, in der Lange Straße 6, ist das Eingangsportal des **Hospital zum Heiligen Geist** ebenfalls sehenswert. 1833-39 von Friedrich Rumpf entworfen, zeigt es die Figuren „Krankheit" und „Genesung" von Eduart Schmidt von der Launitz.

Biegen Sie nach dem Heiliggeist rechts in den nach 1806 entstanden Frankfurter Anlagenring ein und folgen Sie diesem. Zu beiden Seiten sind viele Gebäude aus der Epoche zwischen 1820 und 1860 erhalten geblieben. Sehenswert ist hier das **Odeon,** 1808 als Ausstellungs-Pavillon für die Familie Bethmann erbaut, ist es heute ein Nachtclub.

WALKING TOUR - CLASSICISM

This tour will show you an important period of architecture in Frankfurt. Until 1800 Frankfurt was basically characterised by Gothic buildings. The first onset of Classicism occurred when the city was enlarged after 1780, with the addition of the so-called "Fischerfeld" area and the newly constructed "Paulskirche", the Church of St. Paul.

This tour begins at the **"Paulskirche" (Nr 29).** *In a nutshell, Goethe's comment on the building was: "The right building at the wrong spot". What bothered him was the extreme contrast between the church, which was deemed "modern" at the time, and the Gothic city that surrounded it.*

Cross the Römerberg and walk to **Mainkai 40,** *next to the "Leonhardskirche" (Church of St. Leonhard), there is a small residential building dating back to 1840. It is painted white, just like all of the buildings along the bank of the Main from the period after 1800 that determine the appearance of the Main embankment. The elegant* **"Villa Schlosser"** *(Untermainkai 4) is located further west along the Main. That villa, which was designed by J. F. C. Hess, is one of the extremely popular villas of Frankfurt's upper middle classes.*

Other buildings by Hess located on "Am Untermainkai" are **house numbers 12 - 14.** *This row of buildings is terminated by the Rothschild Palais. Today the 1821 building designed by Hess along with the 1849 addition by F. Rumpf houses the Jewish Museum of Frankfurt.*

Follow the Untermainkai and cross the river via Holbeinsteg. Turn right and alongside the Schaumainkai you get to **Villa Metzler** *(Schaumainkai 15). In 1860 an additional storey with classicistic proportions was added to the summerhouse (1802) for the bankers' family.*

Continue along the course of the Main and change again to its Frankfurt side via the Alte Brücke . "Schöne Aussicht" begins right beyond the bridge. In the back courtyards of the street called **"Hinter der Schönen Aussicht"** *it is possible to discover quite* *a few remains of buildings from around 1800. One example is the house at* **Schützenstraße 1** *dating back to 1820.*

Walk towards the Ignatz-Bubis-Brücke. On the opposite side of the street the most significant example of Classicism - the **Stadtbibliothek** *(City Library)* **(No. 30)** *- is located. The building was designed by J. F. C. Hess, and recently reconstructed by Christoph Mäckler.*

Behind it in Langestraße 6 you can see the entrance portal – built in 1833 - 39 - of the **Hospital zum Heiligen Geist,** *which was designed by Friedrich Rumpf, with sculptural representations depicting "Sickness" and "Recovery" by Eduart Schmidt von der Launitz, which are also worth taking a look at.*

Behind the hospital turn right in the Anlagenring which dates back to 1806. On both sides of this park there are many buildings from the period between 1820 and 1860 that have survived. The **Odeon** *from 1808 is also well worth seeing. It was originally built as an exhibition pavilion for the Bethmann family and is now a popular nightclub.*

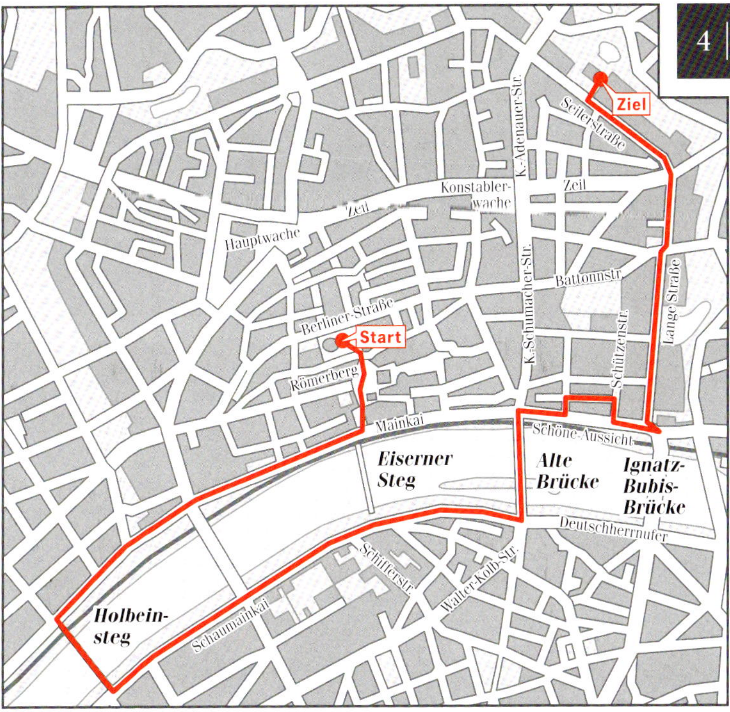

TOUR 4 - Sachsenhäuser Altstadt

Startpunkt für die Tour durch Frankfurts ältesten Stadtteil ist die **Deutschordens-kommende (Nr. 10).** Ende des 12. Jhs. gründete Kuno von Münzenberg hier ein Hospital, das er 1221 dem Deutschen Orden übertrug. Durch dessen Niederlassung und den Bau der Alten Brücke kam es erst zu einer nennenswerten Besiedelung Sachsenhausens.

Von hier aus sind es nur wenige Schritte bis zum Main. Vor sich sehen Sie die **Alte Brücke (Nr. 50)** und den **Portikus (Nr. 91),** halten sich aber rechts und biegen nach wenigen Metern in die Große Rittergasse ein.

Die Straßennamen Kleine und Große Rittergasse sowie Frankensteiner Platz erinnern daran, dass sich im Mittelalter in diesem Teil Sachsenhausens mehrere Ritterhöfe hoher Reichsbeamter befanden. Auf der linken Seite ist ein kleines Stück der früheren Stadtbefestigung erkennbar, zu der einst auch der **Kuhhirtenturm** aus der Zeit um 1490 gehörte (Große Rittergasse 18). Der ehemalige Wachturm wurde 1923–1927 von dem Komponisten Paul Hindemith bewohnt.

Folgen Sie der Gasse bis zum Frankensteiner Platz, wo der **Ritterbrunnen Heiliger Georg,** eine 2007 aufgestellte Kopie des 1788 geschaffenen Pumpbrunnens, einen prominenten Platz erhalten hat.

Noch ein bisschen weiter geradeaus befindet sich rechterhand, etwas zurück-gesetzt – in einem Haus von 1905, dessen Fassade Dekorationselemente des Jugend-stils aufweist – die traditionsreiche Apfelweinwirtschaft **„Lorsbacher Thal“,** die sich seit 1803 bis auf den heutigen Tag in Familienbesitz befindet (Große Rittergasse 49–51).

Am Ende der Gasse schenken Sie dem prächtigen **Hirschbrunnen** von 1796 auf der linken Seite noch einen kurzen Blick, gehen dann zweimal rechts und befinden sich nun in der Klappergasse.

Links steht das **„Steinern' Haus“** aus der Mitte des 15. Jhs., der älteste profane Steinbau des Stadtteils (Klappergasse 3).

Ihm schräg gegenüber spuckt der **Frau Rauscher-Brunnen** von 1961 seine Bewun-derer unbarmherzig nass (vor Klappergasse 10). Frau Rauscher, eine typische Sachsen-häuser Marktfrau, ist die Titelfigur eines in Frankfurt sehr bekannten Fastnachtsliedes, dessen Refrain an der Hauswand neben dem Brunnen abzulesen ist.

Gehen Sie die Klappergasse geradeaus, passieren Sie den Durchgang im Erdgeschoss des vor Ihnen liegenden Hauses und Sie befinden sich auf dem Paradiesplatz. Der dortige **Paradiesbrunnen** von 1786 erinnert an das Verderben, das der Apfel Adam und Eva gebracht hat, während gerade die Sachsenhäuser zu seiner flüssigen Variante, dem Apfelwein (oder korrekt „Ebbelwoi"), ein besonders inniges Verhältnis haben. Bestimmt sind Ihnen längst die ins Kopfsteinpflaster eingelassenen bronzefarbenen Äpfel aufgefallen.

Vom Paradiesplatz aus sind es nur ein paar Schritte zur Paradiesgasse, in die Sie nach links einbiegen, um an den Affentorplatz zu gelangen. Die symmetrischen **Affentorhäuser** zu beiden Seiten der Straße sind klassizistische Wachgebäude von 1811, denn das alte Sachsenhausen endete hier bereits wieder.

Noch einmal sei auf zwei Brunnen aufmerksam gemacht, nämlich auf den **Affenbrunnen** von 1958 hinter dem östlichen Affentorhaus (Affentorplatz 1) und den **Zunftbrunnen** von 1971 hinter dem westlichen (Affentorplatz 2).

Durch die dort beginnende Wallstraße gelangen Sie zur Walter-Kolb-Straße. Überqueren Sie diese und halten Sie sich rechts, bis linker Hand ein paar Stufen zum Haus **Schellgasse 8 (Nr. 9)** führen.

Von hier aus mündet ein kleiner Weg in die Dreikönigsstraße, in der Sie sich nach links wenden und auf die **Dreikönigskirche** stoßen. Die baufällige Kapelle aus der ersten Hälfte des 14. Jhs. wurde 1875–1881 durch eine neugotische Kirche mit 80 Meter hohem Turm ersetzt.

Wenn Sie an ihrem Haupteingang nach rechts gehen und dem Sachsenhäuser Ufer folgen, sind Sie nach kurzem Fußweg wieder am Anfangspunkt des Rundgangs angelangt.

Walking Tour – Medieval Centre of Sachsenhausen

The starting point for this tour through Frankfurt's oldest district is the **"Deutschordenskommende" (No. 10)** *(the commandery of the Teutonic Order). At the end of the 12th century, Kuno von Münzenberg founded a hospital at this location, which he made over to the Teutonic Order in 1221. It was only after the order had established itself here and after the construction of the Old Bridge that there was any appreciable settlement in Sachsenhausen.*

From here it is only a few steps to the Main River. Right in front of you is the **"Alte**

Brücke" (No. 50) *(Old Bridge) and the* **"Portikus" (No. 91).** *But keep to your left and turn onto Große Rittergasse after just a few metres.*

The street names - "Kleine Rittergasse" (i.e. small knight's lane) and "Große Rittergasse" (i.e. large knight's lane) as well as "Frankensteiner Platz" - are reminders that in the Middle Ages several knight's estates owned by high officials of the empire were located here. On the left you can see a small section of the earlier city fortifications, which once also included the **"Kuhhirtenturm"** *(Cowherd Tower) from the period around 1490 (Große Rittergasse 18). The composer Paul Hindemith lived in the former watch tower from 1923-1927.*

Follow the lane until you get to Frankensteiner Platz, where the **"Ritterbrunnen Heiliger Georg"** *(Knight's Fountain of St. George), a copy of the pump fountain created in 1788 that was installed in 2007, is displayed in a prominent position.*

If you continue a little further straight ahead; on the right hand side set back slightly there is a house built in 1905 with a façade embellished with decorative Art Nouveau elements. It houses **"Lorsbacher Thal",** *an apple wine inn with a rich tradition that has been continuously owned by the same family since 1803 until the present day (Grosse Rittergasse 49-51).*

At the end of the lane you can take a brief look at the magnificent **"Hirsch-brunnen"** *fountain from 1796 on the left hand side, and then take two turns to the right to reach Klappergasse.*

On the left is the **"Steinern' Haus"** *(Stone House) dating to the mid 15th century, the oldest secular stone structure in this part of the city (Klappergasse 3).*

Diagonally opposite, the **Frau Rauscher-Brunnen,** *a fountain built in 1961, sprays its admirers with water mercilessly (in front of Klappergasse 10). Frau Rauscher, a typical Sachsenhausen market vendor, is the title figure of a carnival song that is very well known in Frankfurt, the refrain of which is inscribed on the wall of the house next to the fountain.*

Continue straight ahead along Klappergasse, proceeding through the passageway on the ground floor of the house in front of you, and you will reach Paradiesplatz. The **"Paradies-brunnen"** *(Paradise Fountain) from 1786 is a reminder of the downfall that the apple caused for Adam and Eve, while the inhabitants of Sachsenhausen have a very intimate* *relationship with the apple's liquid version, a kind of cider called apple wine (or more correctly "Ebbelwoi"). You have undoubtedly already noticed the bronze-coloured apples that are embedded in the cobblestone pavement.*

From Paradiesplatz it is only a few steps to Elisabethenstraße, where you turn left to get to Affentorplatz. The symmetrical **"Affentorhäuser"** *on both sides of the street are classicistic guard buildings from 1811, because that was where old Sachsenhausen already ended.*

Attention should be drawn to another two fountains, namely the **Affenbrunnen** *built in 1958 behind the eastern Affentorhaus (Affentorplatz 1) and the* **Zunftbrunnen** *built in 1971 behind the western Affentorhaus (Affentorplatz 2).*

Wallstraße, which begins there, will take you to Walter-Kolb-Straße. Cross that street and keep to your right until you reach a stairway with a few steps leading to the house at **Schellgasse 8 (No. 9).**

T4 | 5

From here a small footpath leads to Dreikönigsstraße, where you turn to the left and then arrive at the **"Dreikönigskirche"** *(Church of the Three Kings). The dilapidated chapel built in the first half of the 14th century was replaced in 1875-1881 by a Neo-Gothic church with an 80 metre tower.*

If you walk to the right from the church's main entrance and follow the Sachsenhäuser Ufer along the embankment, a short walk will take you back to the starting point of the walking tour.

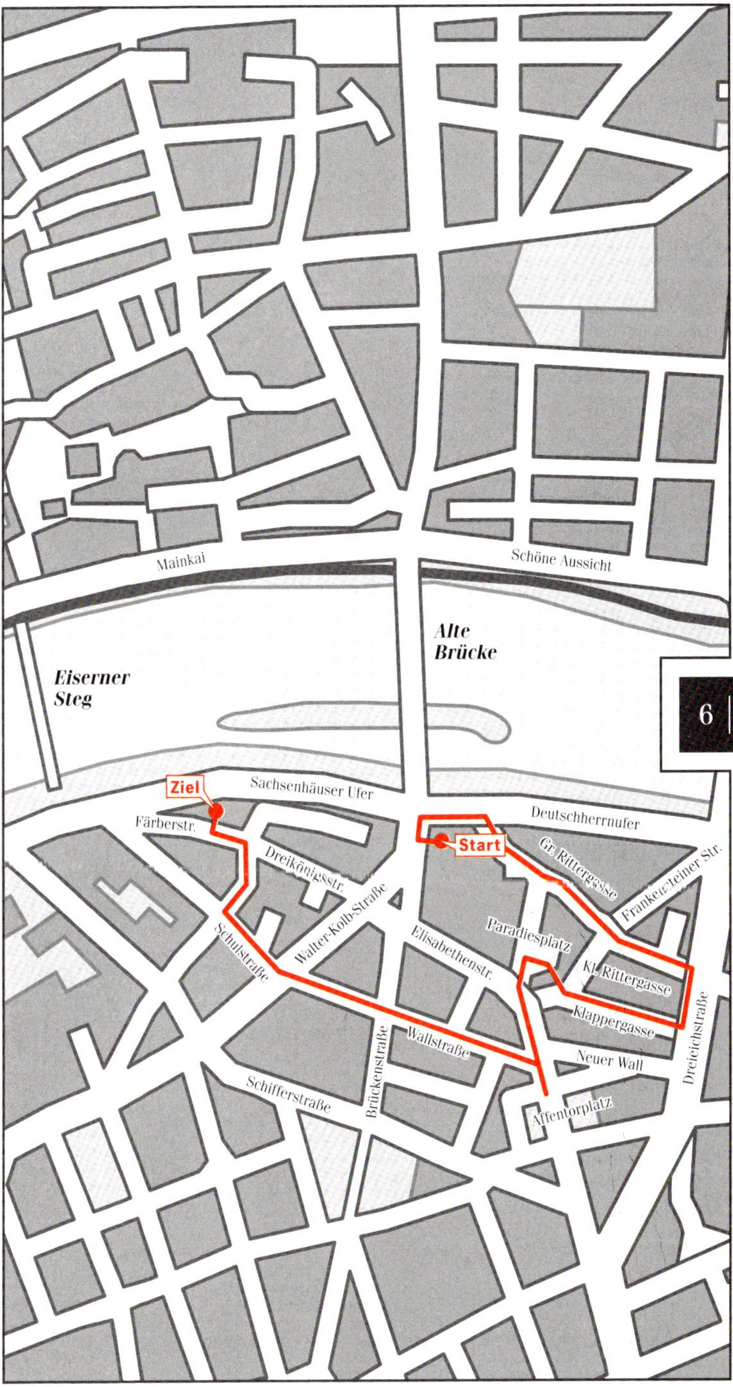
Mainkai
Schöne Aussicht
Alte Brücke
Eiserner Steg
Sachsenhäuser Ufer
Ziel
Start
Deutschherrnufer
Färberstr.
Dreikönigsstr.
Gr. Rittergasse
Frankensteiner Str.
Walter-Kolb-Straße
Paradiesplatz
Elisabethenstr.
Schulstraße
Kl. Rittergasse
Klappergasse
Dreieichstraße
Wallstraße
Brückenstraße
Neuer Wall
Schifferstraße
Affentorplatz

TOUR 5 - Höchster Altstadt

Es bietet sich an, den Spaziergang durch Alt-Höchst am ältesten Gebäude des Stadtteils zu beginnen, der **Justinuskirche (Nr. 1).** Versäumen Sie nicht, auch das Kirchgärtchen auf der Rückseite des Gebäudes zu besichtigen.

Wenn Sie von hier aus Richtung Schlossplatz gehen, liegt auf der rechten Seite ein imposantes steinernes Eckgebäude, das **Alte Rathaus** aus den Jahren 1594–1595 (Allmeygang 8). Der ursprünglich offene Arkadengang im Erdgeschoss ist noch gut zu erkennen.

Auf dem Schlossplatz angekommen, sehen Sie Fachwerkarchitektur aus dem 15. bis 19. Jh.; am berühmtesten ist das ehemalige Gasthaus **„Zum Karpfen“** (Höchster Schlossplatz 11), in dem bereits Dürer, Mozart und Goethe verkehrten (1973 wieder aufgebaut).

Vom **Alten Schloss,** das auf eine Wasserburg des 12. Jhs. zurückgeht, sind heute nur noch der Portalbau, der Bergfried und die nordöstliche Gebäudeecke im Stil der Renaissance erhalten (Höchster Schlossplatz 16). Zur Zeit des Alten Reiches Sitz der Mainzer Amtleute, befindet sich hier heute die Deutsche Stiftung Denkmalschutz.

Durch den ehemaligen **Zollturm** von 1355–1360 gelangen Sie an das gotische **Maintor** mit seinen eindrucksvollen Hochwassermarken. Wenden Sie sich dann nach rechts und laufen Sie an der Stadtmauer entlang, deren Bruchsteinteil aus dem 14. Jh. stammt, während die vorgeblendete Zwingermauer aus Sandstein eine Verstärkung aus den Jahren 1463–1475 ist.

Wenn Sie sich immer an die Stadtbefestigung halten und deren Knick nach Norden mitmachen, gelangen Sie an die Bolongarostraße. Sind Sie nach rechts abgebogen, erblicken Sie gleich auf der linken Seite das **Dalberger Haus** (Bolongarostraße 186), einen früheren Adelshof vom Ende des 16. Jhs.

Schräg gegenüber beginnt die vielleicht schönste Höchster Altstadtgasse, der Burggraben, an dem das **Neue Schloss** vom Anfang des 17. Jhs. und einige sehr schön restaurierte Fachwerkhäuser liegen.

An seinem Ende halten Sie sich links, würdigen an der rechten Ecke kurz das größte Fachwerkgebäude von Höchst, **„Zum Anker“** von 1482 (Bolongarostraße 173), gehen geradeaus in die Wed, an deren Ende das **Greiffenclausche Haus** aus der Zeit um 1590 steht, ein weiterer Adelshof, der einen charakteristischen Renaissancegiebel aufweist (Wed 13).

Genießen Sie nun den Gang durch das idyllische Gässchen Alt-Höchst, wenden Sie sich an seinem Ende nach rechts in die Albanusstraße und gleich wieder links in die Bolongarostraße. Auf der linken Seite steht das **Kronberger Haus** (Bolongarostraße 152). Der im 19. Jh. umgebaute Adelssitz beherbergt heute ein sehenswertes Museum für Höchster Porzellan.

Ihm gegenüber liegen zwei Gebäude des einstigen **Antoniterklosters,** das Spital von 1515–1518 (Bolongarostraße 143) und das Konventsgebäude von 1586 (Bolongarostraße 137–139). Durch die Badstubengasse neben dem alten Spital kommen Sie direkt wieder zum Ausgangspunkt unserer Führung, der Justinuskirche.

Walking Tour – Old Medieval Centre of Höchst

An ideal spot to start the walk through "Alt-Höchst" is the oldest building in this part of the city, **Justinuskirche (No. 1)** *(St. Justinus' Church). Make sure you do not forget to take a look at the tiny church garden at the back of the building.*

When you walk from there to "Schlossplatz" (the castle square), you will see an imposing corner building made of stone on your right, the **Altes Rathaus** *(old city hall) dating to 1594 -1595 (Allmeygang 8). The original open arcade on the ground floor is still easy to recognise*

When you get to Schlossplatz, you will see half-timbered architecture that originated from the 15th to the 19th centuries. The most famous building is the former inn called **"Zum Karpfen"** *(Höchster Schlossplatz 11), where Dürer, Mozart and Goethe were guests (rebuilt in 1973).*

The origin of the **"Altes Schloss"** *(Old Castle) was a 12th century moated castle: the only parts that have survived are the portal section, the keep and the northeastern building corner in the Renaissance style (Höchster Schlossplatz 16). At the time of the Old Empire it was the domicile of the officials from Mainz, today it houses the "Deutsche Stiftung Denkmalschutz", the German foundation for the preservation of historical monuments.*

Passing through the former **"Zollturm"** *(Toll Tower) from 1355 -1360 you will reach the Gothic gate called* **"Maintor"** *with its impressive high water marks. Turn to the right and walk along the city wall. The quarry stone section was built in the 14th century, whereas the bailey wall made of sandstone in front of that is a reinforcement dating back to the years 1463 -1475.*

If you continue along the city fortifications and follow them when they turn a corner towards the north, you will reach Bolongarostraße. Once you turn right, you will immediately see the **"Dalberger Haus"** *(Bolongarostraße 186) on the left, a noble residence dating back to the end of the 16th century.*

Diagonally opposite is the beginning of a narrow lane that is perhaps the most beautiful tiny street in Höchst's medieval centre, Burggraben, where you will see the **Neues Schloss** *(New Castle) from the beginning of the 17th century and several very beautifully restored half-timbered houses.*

At the end of the lane, keep to your left and admire the largest half-timbered building in Höchst on the right hand corner - **"Zum Anker"** *- from 1482 (Bolongarostraße 173). Continue straight ahead into "Wed", at the end of which you will find the* **"Greiffen-clausches Haus"** *dating back to the period around 1590: another noble residence with a characteristic Renaissance gable (Wed 13).*

Now you can enjoy walking through the idyllic lane called Alt-Höchst. At the end, turn to your right onto Albanusstraße and immediately to the left onto Bolongarostraße. The **"Kronberger Haus"** *(Bolongarostraße 152) is on your left. Today that former noble residence, which was remodelled in the 19th century, houses a museum for Höchst porcelain, which is well worth a visit.*

Opposite it there are two buildings belonging to the former **"Antoniterkloster"** *(the monastery of the Hospital Brothers of St. Anthony) the hospital from 1515 -1518 (Bolongarostraße 143) and the convent building from 1586 (Bolongarostraße 137-139). Passing by the old hospital through Badstubengasse you will come right back to the starting point of our tour, the "Justinuskirche".*

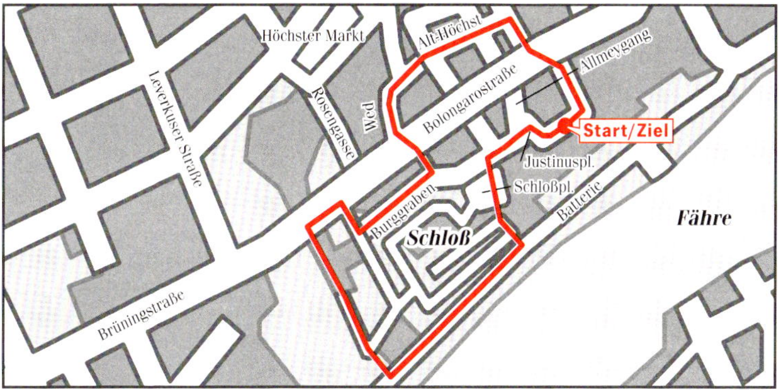

TOUR 6 - Besonderheiten

Der Rundgang beginnt am Römerberg und geht direkt am Gebäude des Römers vorbei in die Limpurger Gasse. Gleich rechts befindet sich ein kleiner **Durchgang in den Römerhof.** Der Durchgang aus dem 15. Jahrhundert wurde vor einigen Jahren liebevoll renoviert. Solche mit Netzgewölbe und Bemalung ausgestatteten Einfahrten waren typisch für das alte Frankfurt.

Folgen Sie der Limpurger Gasse, biegen Sie nach links in die Buchgasse ein. Auf einem Grundstück zwischen Buchgasse und Alte Mainzerstraße befindet sich einer von drei noch erhalten **Renaissance-Treppentürmen.** Häufig standen solche steinernen Treppenhäuser, aus Gründen der Feuersicherheit, in den Höfen der Fachwerkhäuser der Altstadt. Der Gebäuderest wird in den Neubau der Caritas integriert werden.

Gehen Sie die Alte Mainzer Gasse bis zur Seckbächer Gasse entlang, links sehen Sie einen gotischen Durchlass zum Main. Das **Frauenpförtchen** aus der Zeit um 1400 gehört zu den wenigen Resten der gotischen Stadtmauer die Frankfurt zum Main hin schützte. Der Name rührt angeblich daher, dass durch diesen versteckten Einlass die außerhalb der Stadt lebenden Prostituierten unter anderem zum Karmeliter Kloster eingelassen wurden.

Durch die Seckbächer Gasse gelangen Sie zur Weißfrauenstraße. Gehen Sie nach links bis zur Neuen Mainzer Straße und folgen Sie dieser nach rechts. An der Ecke Kaiserstraße **(Kaiserstraße 25)** sehen Sie ein Geschäftshaus einer ganz anderen Epoche. Der Frankfurter Architekt Paul Wallot entwarf dieses reich dekorierte Gebäude 1875. Von Wallot stammt auch der Reichstag in Berlin.

Weiter in der Neuen Mainzer Straße geht es zum **ehemaligen Bankhaus Pfeifer Belli** (Hausnummer 55). Der zierliche klassizistische Bau von 1830 bildet einen besonderen Kontrast zu den Hochhäusern der Umgebung und vermittelt eine Vorstellung der historischen Neubebauung entlang der alten Wallanlage nach 1806. Ein rückseitiger Garten gehört ebenfalls zum Gesamtkomplex.

Gehen Sie nach links in die Junghofstraße und folgen Sie rechts der Taunusanlage. Nach der Alten Oper können Sie nach links einen Abstecher in den **Rothschildpark** unternehmen. Darin finden Sie einen um 1830 erbauten Turm, der die damals populäre Ruinenarchitektur dokumentiert. Der Turm war nie in Funktion und von Anbeginn verschlossen.

Von der Alten Oper nach rechts folgen Sie der Bockenheimer Anlage. Sie passieren einen Rest der historischen **Barocken Bastionen.** Diese Bastionen wurden ab 1630 der gotischen Stadtmauer vorgelagert.

Hinter dem ehemaligen Stadtbad erreichen Sie das **Nebbien'sche Gartenhaus.** Das 1810 von Johann Jakob Nebbien samt Garten und Brunnen errichtete Gebäude ist ein Beleg für die damalige Gestaltung der überflüssig gewordenen Stadtbefestigung.

Am Eschenheimer Tor vorbei gelangen Sie in die Eschenheimer Anlage. An der Einmündung der Sternstraße sehen Sie das **Maurische Haus.** Seinen morgenländischen Stil verdankt dieses Gebäude, 1857 vom Frankfurter Maurermeister Johann Friedrich Weinsperger errichtet, angeblich einer unglücklichen Liebesaffäre eines Frankfurter Bürgers zu einer orientalischen Schönheit.

Ein kleines Stück zurück und Sie erreichen über die Krögerstraße die Bleichstraße. Folgen Sie dieser nach links bis zur **Peterskirche (12).** Über den Peterskirchhof gelangen Sie zur Stephanstraße. Folgen Sie dieser nach rechts und biegen Sie in die Stiftstraße ein. Mit den Häusern **Stiftstraße 6 und 8 - 10** sehen Sie zwei der wenigen in Frankfurt gebauten Jugendstil-Gebäude. Während Frankfurts Bauboom um 1900 bevorzugte man die große gründerzeitliche Geste.

Der Stiftstraße und der Hasengasse folgend kommen Sie zur **Töngesgasse,** wo sich im Hof der Hausnummer 36 der heute als Museum für den Frankfurter Mundartdichter Friedrich Stoltze genutzte Renaissance-Treppenturm von 1600 befindet. Vielleicht hat Ihnen dieser Rundgang einen Eindruck dafür vermittelt, wie Stoltze zu seinen berühmten Zeilen kam:
Es is kaa Stadt uff der weite Welt, die merr wie mei Frankfort gefällt, un es will merr net in mein Kopp enei, wie kann nor e Mensch net von Frankfort sei!

Walking Tour – Special Sights

The tour begins at the "Römerberg" and proceeds directly past the buildings of the "Römer" (Frankfurt's city hall) into Limpurger Gasse. Immediately on the right hand side in Limpurger Gasse there is a **small passageway leading into the Römerhof courtyard.** *This passageway, which dates back to the 15th century, was lovingly restored a few years ago. Gateways like this with reticulated vaulting and painted decoration were quite typical for Frankfurt of old.*

Follow the Limpurger Gasse then turn left into Buchgasse. There, between Buchgasse and Alte Mainzerstraße you will find one of the three surviving **Renaissance stair towers.** *This type of stone staircase was quite common in the courtyards of the half-timbered houses of the old medieval centre for fire safety reasons. The vestiges of the building are being integrated into the new building of Caritas, a Roman-Catholic charity.*

Walk along Mainzer Gasse until you reach Seckbächer Gasse where you will see a Gothic footpath leading to the Main River on your left. The gate called **Frauenpförtchen** *dates back to the period around 1400. It is one of the few vestiges of the Gothic city wall that protected Frankfurt on the side facing the Main. Ostensibly, it ist called Frauenpförtchen because Prostitutes living outside the city used this hidden entrance to pay secret visits to the Karmeliter Kloster.*

Walk through Seckbächer Gasse until you get to Weißfrauenstraße. Now turn left into the Neue Mainzer Straße and follow the street turn right. At the corner of Kaiserstraße the **business premises at No. 25** *are from a very different period. The Frankfurt architect Paul Wallot designed this richly decorated building in 1875. Wallot also designed the Reichstag building in Berlin.*

By continuing along Neue Mainzer Straße you will reach the **former Bankhaus Pfeifer Belli** *(No. 55). This diminutive classicistic structure built in 1830 is in stark contrast to the high-rise buildings that surround it. The building gives an idea of what the historical new construction built after 1806 along the old ramparts was like. This building also included a garden facing the ramparts.*

Now turn left in the Junghofstraße and follow the Taunusanlage on your right hand side. After passing the Alte Oper you can make a short detour to the **Rothschildpark.** *Here you take a look at a Tower built in 1830 which represents the then very popular so-called ruined architecture. The tower was never used and never opened.*

On the right hand side of the Alte Oper you walk in the Bockenheimer Anlage and pass the remains of the historical **baroque bastions.** *They were built in front of the Gothic city wall as of 1630.*

Behind the former Stadtbad Mitte swimming pool the **Nebbien'sche Gartenhaus** *is located. It was built along with its garden and a well by Johann Jakob Nebbien in the year 1810. The house is an example of how the by then unnecessary city's fortification could be reused.*

Past the Eschenheimer Tor you reach Eschenheimer Anlage. Where Sternstraße begins you can see the **Maurische Haus,** *which was built in 1857 by the Frankfurt master constructor Johann Friedrich Weinsperger. Ostensibly, it was built in an oriental style because of an unhappy romance of a wealthy Frankfurt citizen and an exotic beauty.*

Go back a few metres, pass Krögerstraße and go into Bleichstraße. Walk this street along until you reach the **Peterskirche (12)** *on your left hand side. Past its churchyard you get to Stephanstraße. From there turn right in the* **Stiftstraße. Its numbers 6 and 8 to 10** *are two of the very few Art Nouveau buildings that were ever built in Frankfurt. During Frankfurt's construction boom around 1900 there was a preference for the ostentatious Wilhelminian style.*

Following Stiftstraße and Hasengasse you arrive in **Töngesgasse.** *Here, in the courtyard of house number 36, you will find a Renaissance staircase tower dating back to 1600, which is currently used as the museum for Frankfurt's dialect author Friedrich Stoltze.*

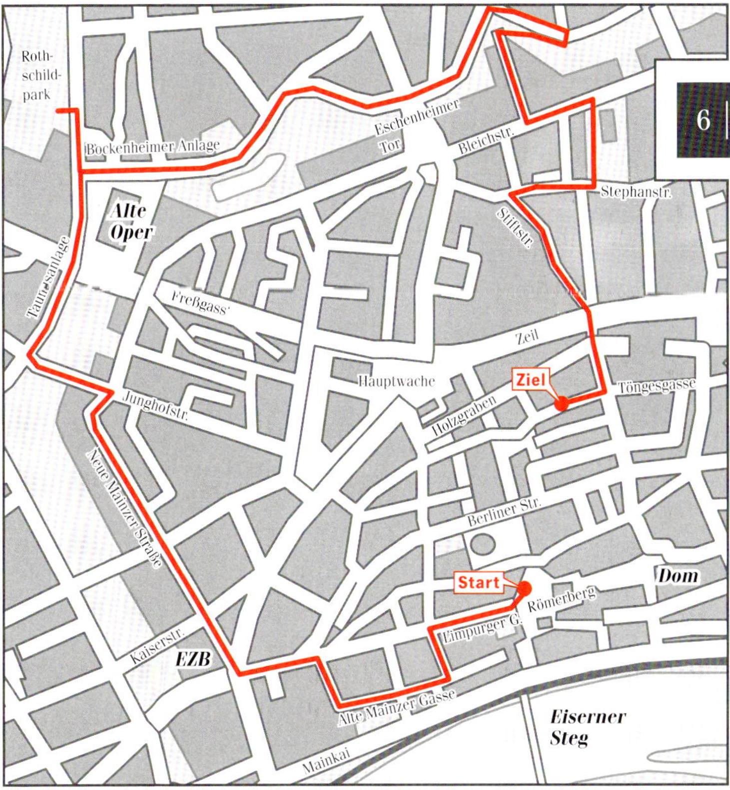
Roth-
schild-
park
Bockenheimer Anlage
Eschenheimer
Tor
Bleichstr.
Stephanstr.
Stiftstr.
Alte
Oper
Freßgass'
Zeil
Hauptwache
Ziel
Töngesgasse
Holzgraben
Junghofstr.
Neue Mainzer Straße
Berliner Str.
Start
Dom
Römerberg
Limpurger G.
Kaiserstr.
EZB
Alte Mainzer Gasse
Eiserner
Steg
Mainkai

Die 100 Gebäude in alphabetischer Reihenfolge

Gebäude, Plätze und Sehenswürdigkeiten der Touren in alphabetischer Reihenfolge

Die Autoren

Silke Wustmann ist Historikerin und Stadtführerin in Frankfurt am Main und kennt diese Stadt wie kaum eine andere. In unterschiedlichen Kostümen, ob Bürgersfrau oder Marktweib, bringt sie vielen Besuchern die Geschichte der Mainmetropole näher. Von ihr sind im B3 Verlag bereits die „Frankfurter Liebespaare“ als Buch und Hörbuch erschienen.

Christian Setzepfandt ist Kunsthistoriker und organisiert seit 30 Jahren Führungen zu unterschiedlichen Themen in und um Frankfurt. Er betreibt das Büro Kultours. Von ihm sind bereits die Bücher „Geheimnisvolles Frankfurt“ und der „Architekturführer Frankfurt am Main“ erschienen.